A WRITER'S GUIDE TO WIZZLEY

BY

JO HARRINGTON

Copyright © 2013 Jo Harrington
All rights reserved.
ISBN: 1484088034
ISBN-13: 978-1484088036

This eBook is dedicated to Sareyva, who walked with me every single step of the way. I'll never forget what you did for me. Thank you.

Contents

Foreword by Achim 'ChefKeem' Thiemermann

1	What is Wizzley?	1
2	Who Are You? And Why Should We Listen to You?	3
3	The Bottom Line	7
4	Creating your Wizzley Account	9
5	Monetizing Wizzley	21
6	In the Beginning...	28
7	Creating a Page on Wizzley	37
8	Is Wizzley a Content Farm?	53
9	The Future for Wizzley	56

Bonus Material   59

Foreword

What does Google want? Or, better - what do I have to do to get my stuff on the front pages of Google Search?

Those are the main questions that thousands of online authors ask themselves every day. Then they fire up their latest keyword tool, spend hours on research, read up on any "new rules" regarding keyword density, bolding, italicizing, and maximum numbers of outbound links. And then - with spinning heads and a great deal of doubt - they finally publish a piece that reads like an episode of any popular network TV show: Little substance but lots of self-serving interruptions.

And then there's Jo Harrington.

She didn't think about any of the above. (She didn't know about these things, back then when she started writing online.) Jo asked herself only one question: Which stories in my life touch me so deeply that I have to share them with the world? And then she wrote. And wrote. And wrote.

And then the readers came. And came. And kept coming by the thousands.

Apparently, with her own question, Jo had found the answer to the very first question on this page.

When Jo sinks her teeth into something that interests her (like vampires), she won't let go until her thirst for knowledge is completely satisfied. And that's exactly how she approached the issue of making money with her work. She studied all the materials, and then she shaped everything into the best possible user experience. She takes her readers by the hand and leads them from value (information) to more value (recommendation). Her ads don't interrupt - they complement her content. And value sells!

Jo is a natural-born online author. Her success proves it. Thank God she's a generous soul, as well. In this book, she shares everything she knows about our craft - from page-building instructions to exquisite writing tips, specifically (but not exclusively) for Wizzley authors.

Whether you are a beginner or an established writer - it's a fun and inspiring read that will make you a better author, possibly even in ways you have never considered before.

I love it.

Achim Thiemermann (chefkeem)
Co-Founder/Community Manager
wizzley.com

What is Wizzley?

Wizzley is an online magazine. Its topics are varied; and its authors come from all over the world. They bring with them a passion and an enthusiasm so rarely seen anymore, in times of recession. You could be one of them.

Wizzley authors fall into two distinct categories, though the two are not mutually exclusive. There are those here to make money. Their articles attract commission from the advertizements placed on the page. There are others who merely want a platform from which their voices may be heard. They are writing because they have a message to convey, or information to impart. This category includes those who have no option but to write. They craft words in the same way as a violinist teases melodies from the strings. They write because they are writers.

There is a place for all of these people on Wizzley. The mix is what makes it a beautiful compository of pages on the internet. Readers are lured to the website by one link. They leave an hour or two later, having been side-tracked into exploring many others. The stories are there. The recommendations. The reviews. The warnings. The opinion pieces. The biographies. The news. It is all too easy to immerse yourself in reading them, especially as the emphasis is on value. Nothing sub-standard or thin is allowed to remain on Wizzley. Their authors would be invited to expand upon what they've written.

However the real world always beckons. It's the sales figures which really underline the reason to be writing here for many authors. There are always bills to be paid. Wizzley is a place in which to make an income working from home. Each article represents one more chance to create one. All articles together build and build until the funds flow into the coffers. That's both the theory and the

actuality.
    Can you write? If so, then Wizzley awaits you. Come on in.

Who Are You? And Why Should We Listen to You?

I'm nobody and you shouldn't.

I'm also Jo Harrington and a Wizzley author. Call the above my own personal backlash against all of those over-the-top e-mails and websites, where people you have never heard of tell you how they are the greatest entrepreneur known to humanity. They are the writers' writer, the consultants' consultant and possibly the president's president, only they're too modest to say the last.

After picking through reams of self-glorification, you reach the end without a single insight into anything much.

Except where to buy the eBook. It has secrets, you know. It can tell you how to be the most read author on the internet. *And you've still never heard of them!*

I'd prefer you to consider me as someone met on a cliff-top walk, who's familiar with the terrain. I can tell you where the path has crumbled and mark your map with viewpoints of outstanding natural beauty. But I'm not going to tell you to follow my route.

Nor should I. Writing is all about finding your own voice; and affecting mine will be like putting on a silly accent. No-one will take you seriously. Instead I will present a few options, with much encouragement to find more of your own. I'll add in the rationale, all of the whys and wherefores, so you can make educated decisions of your own, based on what works for you. I'll tell you what works for me. I'll point out what works for other people too. At the end of it, you'll hopefully see your own way quite clearly, if only the starting point.

I arrived at Wizzley over a year ago, and I've written as many articles as were days in that time. I came as a novice, learning my craft; but that's not necessarily a reason to dismiss me out of hand. Blessed are the newcomers, because they will press every button, try every course, experiment with options which the experience weary veterans swear will never work, and end up discovering new ways of doing things. Of course, it helps that this quest was undertaken within a community filled with knowledgable people willing to share their tips; and to rein me in, when I was heading straight for a precipice.

In many ways, I think that put me into a charmed position. The best of all worlds. And that Fool's Journey has apparently paid off.

Here's the bit where I give my credentials. Please skip over it, if you couldn't care less about someone you've never heard of. Because if you had heard of me, then you wouldn't need to know.

- o I have received the most Editor's Choice Awards on Wizzley. They currently stand at fourteen.
- o My articles habitually make the front page to the point of embarrassment. At the moment of writing, there are eighteen Wizzles there. Thirteen of them were penned by me.
- o My last article was listed on page one of the Google SERPs, within an hour of being published, for just about every relevant keyword and phrase that I could think of to check.
- o Another of my articles went a bit viral and received nearly 80,000 hits within a twenty-four hour period. It was on the front page of Reddit.
- o I was given the rare opportunity to tour a major gaming studio based on one of my articles about it.
- o I've placed second and first respectively in

two different Wizzley writing competitions.

So yes, I'm not doing too badly for someone just starting out. My actual traffic statistics are included on the next page. I've done a lot with my first twelve months on Wizzley; and now I'm going to hopefully help you do the same.

Call it passing it forward, in recompense for all the people who reached back for me during that time, and nurtured me while I found my voice.

I am the Wizzley writers' writer, you know. No? Ok, let's move swiftly on.

My Wizzley Progress

These are my statistics from my first year at Wizzley, so that you may judge for yourself if my advice is worth reading.

Pages	Page Impressions	Unique Visitors	7 Days	30 Days	90 Days
50	17,669	10,953	3,096	8,997	10,953
100	56,193	32,780	4,505	16,000	32,030
150	139,496	82,755	6,243	19,749	60,055
200	211,236	125,392	5,090	18,992	59,353
250	330,975	228,391	7,002	95,754	132,664
300	393,853	267,255	7,379	30,535	147,208
350	442,556	299,523	9,211	38,142	164,767
400	562,441	379,239	7,913	33,192	87,455

The Bottom Line

Everybody needs to make a living, no matter how squeamish you are about asking people for hard cash. Even the most passionate of writers needs bread on the table. So let's get the questions about that old filthy lucre out of the way.

There is no hierarchy on Wizzley, beyond the effort that you put in and achieve for yourself. If you have written for websites before where there's a sliding scale of payments, based upon author rank, then be prepared to embrace equality.

Wizzley does not pay out any money. It facilitates you getting payment for yourself. Each page that you write can be monetized in a variety of ways, with ready-built modules to help you display products in the most attractive and effective ways possible. In addition, the site will automatically insert hot-spot ads from Google or Chitika.

All newcomers arrive to a 50/50 split with Wizzley. This means that for half of the time every single monetized element on that page will be ready to make money for you. The other half, it will be making money for the site. The recipient changes on each fifth page refresh.

To put this even more simply, imagine that you have just published an article and the alert has gone out to your e-mail list. The first five people who come to read it are your potential customers. The second five are customers of Wizzley. The third five are yours; and so on.

However, though it may seem like a fair split, the odds are actually against the site itself! Because Chitika displays for my pages and Google Adsense for Wizzley's, I've been able to observe this cycle in action. The first visitor is always mine. In fact, I've sometimes had to refresh several times before Adsense is shown. The benefit is negligible compared to the hundreds or thousands who will eventually turn up to read, but the odds are in your favor.

Then there are the referral links. Here is mine: http://wizzley.com/?pr=1976

If you join Wizzley through that link, I will gain 10% of the monetization on your articles for all time. This does not come out of your 50%, but the site's share. So now the cut is: 50% to you, 40% to Wizzley and 10% to me. Naturally I would be very grateful if you did register through that referral link!

Another change in your favor occurs with the advent of your 50th article going live. Fifty is so often seen as the magic number in online writing platform articles, as things tend to happen. On Wizzley, that is the cut shifting to 55% to you. That extra five percent may not seem like much, but those pennies and cents do add up.

Finally, at your 100th article, the percentage moves further into your favor for one last time. Now it's 60% to you and 40% to Wizzley; or 30% to Wizzley and 10% to the person who referred you.

As for where all those riches are coming from, that's better dealt with in the next chapter: Creating your Wizzley Account.

Creating Your Wizzley Account

http://wizzley.com/?pr=1976

I just thought I'd leave that referral link lying about there. This is my utterly transparent attempt to become a savvy marketing entrepreneur. Now all you need to do is register with it, then make millions from your articles. Then we can both retire. It's worth a try anyway.

(Incidentally, if you really don't want to credit me, then remove the '?/pr=1976'. Then you can register without any referral and maintain the initial 50-50 split with Wizzley. The management there will love you!)

Choosing a Name

Your first task is to decide upon your professional writing name. Wizzley allows no spaces, so if it isn't one word, you need to add a hyphen, dash or anything else to make it fit. I merely removed the space. Jo Harrington became JoHarrington and we all know where we stand there!

While this is all new and exciting, it is best to pause for a moment and contemplate the bigger picture. If you are an unknown writer now, then you may not be for long. As your fame and popularity spreads across cyber-space, do you really want an unsuitable pseudonym? Later down the line, your Wizzley portfolio might be an item to add to your resume. An air of professionalism has to prevail then. Having a name like, say, DogPukeDoggieDog may be highly amusing now; but not so much when you're trying to craft a serious article about fine porcelain or child abuse. It certainly won't be at all funny if you're attempting to gain credibility with your readers or a prospective employer.

In those circumstances, copying me and using your

real name would be perfect. But it isn't the only option.

What will you be writing about? If you have a niche topic in mind, then a moniker which reflects it might be appropriate. There is somebody on Wizzley called XmasDecs. As you have probably guessed, his articles are all about Christmas Decorations. There is another who owns an art gallery in the real world. She has chosen to write under the name of that gallery, LakeErieArtists. It's all publicity for those who might walk through her door.

Or maybe you are already well-known under a pen-name. There is nothing wrong with that. You can be sure that if Mark Twain was alive today to sign up to Wizzley, he wouldn't be there as SamClemens. Not if he wanted maximum internet traffic anyway.

Back in the digital stone age, one Wizzley author began writing under the name of Hospitalera for reasons too obscure to go into here. Internet eons have passed and she is now known across several blogs, forums and a website as that name. It links her disparate work together and provides continuity for her readership. Her authority as a writer is all bound up in that identifying label, Hospitalera. Therefore it is a pity that she made a sentimental error in registering on Wizzley as Sam. She regrets it now, but they were all good reasons at the time.

So reflect for a while on what image you wish to convey with your name. What is its purpose? And whom does it serve? Then pick one accordingly.

Entering Wizzley as a Registered Author

After entering your name and e-mail address (the latter is an accountability safe-guard), plus password, you will next be asked to confirm that you've read the Terms and Conditions.

Please read that with due diligence, then come into the Wizzley forum and tell us what it said. You can be sure that it'll be news for the majority of us. Who ever reads those things before something goes wrong? For the record, it's a pretty standard and fair ToS. It simply states that your confirmation represents a legal and binding agreement that Wizzley now owns you body and soul; and the management can sell your grandmother into slavery, if you spam the forum or bring the site into disrepute. Standard stuff. Just click past it.

Welcome to Wizzley! Nip and follow JoHarrington, if you like. I'll get an alert and immediately follow you straight back. That's one friend made!

But all of this is looking a little bare until we fill in your profile. As well as adding some substance to your page, it's also an important factor in calculating your author rank. I'll get onto all of that in a later chapter, so just note that it is so for now.

Click on your name, on the upper toolbar, and you will see revealed the pull-down menu that will own your Wizzley writing career from now on. Find 'Settings' on the list and click on it. Time to integrate your life into the site.

Profile Information

With the exception of the honorific, everything that you write in the boxes here will be displayed to the public from your Wizzley page. Therefore, if you've chosen a super secret user pseudonym to thwart the agencies after you, don't mess it up now by typing in your real name.

I was boring. My username is JoHarrington. My profile name is Ms Jo Harrington. That's practically what you'd find on my birth certificate, but I *am* aiming for the professional look here.

Of course, you don't have to add anything at all, though your readers may wonder what you have to hide. The more information that you include, the more like a real person you appear; and that can only be good for cultivating a returning readership and conveying a thin veneer of authority over your work. But there is a pay-off risk too, and now might be the perfect juncture to talk about internet security.

Human nature isn't always kind. You don't need to prove your common sense and compassion to acquire a wireless connection. Humanity has always had the capacity for great evil and great good, often exhibiting both at the same time without fear of contradiction. The majority are neither. We are all of the shades of grey in between, depending upon the time of day, the weather or whatever other whim can delight or distress us.

Unfortunately an avatar and words on the page do not always converge into a real, thinking, feeling person, in the perception of trolls or those with anger management issues. In the extremely unlikely event that one of your articles inspires a machete wielding psychopath to come looking for you, how much information do you want to give them to go on?

For this reason (or to keep an online identity separate from the real world for a less paranoid rationale), some choose not to give away too much here at all. I've left my home city blank, so that would mean pursuers have to search the entire British Isles. The Wizzley team are also internet safety minded, insofar as your birthday is displayed only as your age; and all else is asked and rendered in the most generic terms.

A good compromise is to create an online persona which appears to be plausibly real. You get the benefits of a real looking name, with all the rounded facts around it, which humanizes you in the minds of readers. But none of it could be followed back to your doorstep.

Of course, I took none of this advice. My digital paper trail is a DOXer's wet dream. But my duty here is done. Take your risks or your precautions as you see fit, your choices are all your own.

Choosing a Profile Image

One of the first tips that I was ever given by a veteran online writer concerned my avatar. I was told that a writer whose face can be viewed gains trust and authority more quickly. It's because we have all been programmed from infancy to focus on faces. It's probably in our genes. Faces mean warm milk, a cuddle or having our diapers changed. Though probably not now that we're adults. No faces mean that we've been left alone with the monsters under the bed. An inner instinct rings the alarm, 'Do not like', and that's it! We're not trusting this writer to tell us all about whatever it is that they're waffling on about.

At least that is the theory. It sounds legit. Plus a mug-shot does look more professional. They have them in banks and airports. It's a cultural thing.

There is another, relatively marginal consideration. Google is currently on a quest to make all of us use our real names and show our real faces on profile pictures. Their reasons are nefarious and all to do with proper data collection, so that they can serve us perfectly targeted advertisements (and hand over accurate information to whichever government decides that we are terrorists). As this is all so very blatant, most of the internet has responded with a resounding no.

However, there is actually a carrot in there for online writers. If our profiles are linked up to Google Plus, and if our avatars depict a human face, then there's a possibility that said avatar will appear alongside article links in the Google SERPs. That helps our URLs stand out from the masses and attract more readers accordingly. Worth it? You decide.

That said, this is the internet and avatars have long been any pretty picture that the owner had on their hard-drive at the time. A friend of mine on a gaming forum caused uproar when he changed his cartoon frog of five years' standing, to something more representative of his advancing years. We'd all grown to recognize and know that frog. In some weird, warped way, it was him; even while none of us actually believed he looked like that.

The lesson here is that it's familiarity and precedent that truly builds trust. That banker can stick as many professional portraits of himself as he wants on the wall, but he's still a banker. None of us are going to trust him with anything more important than our life savings.

As long as your profile picture is in no way offensive, and it's something that you can live with forever, then I now see no reason why you can't use anything that fits. Wizzley recommends the smiling face, but only for the reasons already stated. You could just as easily choose something which mirrors your niche. The aforementioned XmasDecs is represented by a Christmas tree covered in lights.

Though you are able to change your avatar at any time, I do strongly recommend that you do not. Never underestimate that powerful human capacity for noting patterns and inwardly recoiling when they disappear. My friend was somehow lessened when his frog went away. He eventually had to bow to public pressure to reinstate it. Your readers won't bother with all of that. They'll just quietly slip away.

Continuity is key. So pick your picture carefully!

Oh No! My Profile Image Won't Load!!!

This is one of the most frequent calls for help on the Wizzley forum! We get to know so many newcomers helping them out with loading their avatar.

It's usually one of two things: Is your photograph over 5MB? If so, then it's too big and Wizzley can't load it. If you resize your image, then all will be well. It won't stay at 5MB by the way. The uploader resizes it to a much more sensible 100KB. Has your photograph got a transparent layer? Those pulled off the internet or from the memory cards of good digital cameras often have, but Wizzley can't upload it like that.

To fix it, you could faff around in a photo editing program; or you could just open your picture in Paint, save it as a .jpg, then smirk as you're warned that it will lose its transparent layer. Gleefully agree to that and then upload it into Wizzley again.

The only time I recall it not being either of them, Wizzley was going through routine maintenance and it caused a temporary glitch. The writer waited ten minutes, cleared their cache and tried again. It uploaded first time.

Penning Your Profile's Mini-Biography

I have just randomly clicked onto your Wizzley profile page. You have about five seconds to hook me, before I get bored and wander off again. This, to my mind, is the primary point of the words written in the 'About Me' box, which are then reproduced in your profile's header.

A secondary major use is to inform the genuinely half-interested reader, who is browsing through profiles like other people inspect bookcases in a library. What section are they in now? Will there be anything here worth exploring further? You have more time to sell yourself to this person, but still only limited words in which to do so.

There is no Wizzley gold standard as to how this is done; and perhaps there shouldn't be. Here, more than anywhere, is the personality imprinted upon the profile. There are those who write in third person, and others in first. Some utter a curt couple of words, as if begrudging having to write anything in there at all. Others compose mini essays, which curl around their avatar and require the reader to click onto it and scroll, in order to finally finish the sentence.

I went for somewhere in the middle. Historian, Pagan, gamer and geek, Jo Harrington has been writing since she was old enough to guide a pen. That's it. It tells you five things about me, which are hopefully random enough to attract at least a passing glance. I have articles which back up all of those assertions, and they are all true. There was also plenty more that I left out, mostly because it scanned really nicely as it was.

Plus it was the perfect length to render the formatting of my header clean and tidy. That was my main consideration. It was the geek in me trained not to clutter up pages to the extent that a casual glance can't appreciate the aesthetics. It looks pretty, so they read. It was the way I was taught to design web pages, rather than anything that the writer has brought into play.

Your profile's mini-biography should reflect your own voice and personality, but do think long and hard about its purpose. You may discern a different role than any that I've identified. Don't be afraid to check out everyone else's profiles on Wizzley to see what they did. What did you warm to? What turned you off? What were the common factors in each of those cases? What can you take from that bit of research? How will you write your own?

If it helps, then think of each element of your profile like game pieces sitting on a board. What is your ultimate goal? And how best can you position your pieces to attain that goal?

Nothing on Wizzley, in all its design and framework, is a throw-away accident. The Wizzley team avidly read every scrap of insight into current SEO best practices (so that we don't have to). The site is optimized to the hilt and it's already our greatest asset, excepting the actual content. It's up to us to take random elements, like the mini-biography, and decide how best to make them really work for us.

Besides, you don't have to get everything in. There's room for a Wizzography right underneath! (Which I'll deal with in a separate chapter.)

Social Networking Links

Just a few years ago, you could drop a half-hearted, barely coherent couple of paragraphs into an online writing site. Then walk away and, within a day or two, you would have earned enough money to retire onto your own tropical island, with a mansion to call home.

At least that's the impression you get, listening to the reminiscences of those in this job for half a decade or more. They're possibly a little misty eyed as they speak, but it's hard to tell, hidden as they are behind such deeply rose-tinted glasses.

Nevertheless, there is a kernel of truth in it all.
Even a year ago, when I was arriving on the scene, there was still an overwhelming over-dependence upon Google. The company was viewed as both the primary provider of internet traffic, and the cash-cow. All of the earliest advice I was ever given revolved around how best to serve this capricious master; and what could be sacrificed to stop it smiting us all. Even Panda didn't fatally shake the faith. It took several months and then Penguin to do that. Yet even on the other side of those search engine changes, there are still writers who you feel might possibly offer up their first born, if it would appease Matt Cutts.

Meanwhile, like waking from a long dream of Serfdom, everyone else has turned their attention to the social networking sites. If you want your articles to be read, then you have to have a presence upon them. Our readers live there, with potentially many millions more to follow. For online writers, this is a much healthier, symbiotic relationship than that which went before.
Previously, if I wanted people to find and read my work, I

had to wait for Google's spiders to crawl the site. Then it was a case of hoping that I hadn't fallen foul of some algorithm tweak this week and thus dropped twenty pages in the SERPs.

Now, I have much more control over putting my article under the noses of potential readers. I can send it out into the social network the instant that it's published; then send it again at a later date. Moreover, and perhaps most significantly of all, this isn't just one site, one entity, one company's business strategies. One article might do well on Pinterest; another on Twitter; and a third on StumbleUpon. I judge my success these days not on the internet traffic per se, but the variety of sources. If Facebook went down tomorrow, we'd still have Reddit. If Digg changed its policies to be antagonistic towards self-promotion, then we'd ignore it in favor of Rebelmouse. That makes for much better job security.

For this reason alone, it's worth registering for each of the big sites (Facebook, Twitter, StumbleUpon, Google Plus and LinkedIn), then adding your details into Wizzley.

That latter is for sheer convenience. After you've published one of your articles, a box of icons appears on the page. They link directly to your own social networking profiles. It's a matter of click, click, click and they're all publicized, in a sudden burst of transitory billboarding. However, you can just as easily be on the social networking channels without involving Wizzley at all.

I have chosen not to connect my Facebook account and Wizzley. This is because of the second use for filling in the social networking information in your settings. It activates the links in your public profile, so that readers could come and find you there. Great! I'll chat with them all over a nice cup of tea and several Tweets. But not Facebook. My family are on there, as are friends dating back to my schooldays, through to last week's forum buddies. They are all dropping the kind of personal information about me that I can't control. Certain pictures of me from the Glastonbury Festival are not going to do wonders for my professional image.

The concern is in the other direction too. I don't really frequent Facebook too often. My articles are posted there via Hootsuite and a linked up Twitter stream. I could have readers befriend me, who then sit for weeks wondering why I haven't responded to their PM. It would look rude and therefore not a situation that I want to foster.

Meet me on Twitter instead.

Forum Signature and Page Footer

Wizzley has a very vibrant and helpful community. While we're forever in and out of each other's private message inboxes, and in the comments of articles, the main meeting place is the Wizzley forum. There, conversations from the serious to the mundane take place every hour of the day.

Your messages can, and should, contain a signature. Many Wizzley authors use this to publicize links to their Zazzle stores or personal web-sites. The rationale is two-fold. Your fellow writers can read too. They might come and visit! But more importantly, those messages are scanned and catalogued by the search engines. There's an off-chance that you might find another reader or ten, if someone should stumble upon one of your posts.

Once you have filled this in and saved the settings, it might be nice to pop into the Wizzley forum. There is a category there especially for newcomers to say hello. It could be your chance to start making valuable friends amongst this knowledgeable community.

The page footer appears at the bottom of every one of your articles, but hidden away at the foot of all of the comments. It's less likely to be seen down there than your forum signature, but always a nice find for a reader suddenly spotting it. I personally haven't used this yet. Those who do tend to add quotations or other personal identifiers.

It's another piece on your game-board. What will you do with it?

Monetizing Wizzley

You are now at the stage in your settings where the serious business of securing your wages comes in. If you already have affiliate accounts with any or all of those available at Wizzley, then feel free to start adding your codes and links.

If you have not, then I would counsel caution while you have nothing in your gallery. These companies will be coming to evaluate you as a publisher. They are not going to be too impressed with blank pages. I know two people now who were denied by Google Adsense for precisely this reason. I know that it's frustrating, but get five or ten articles written and out, then start applying for affilate accounts. Those pages will be retrospectively monetized anyway.

Products and other adverts placed on your Wizzley pages (Wizzles in my parlance) is how you and Wizzley make money. You may not smother your articles in them. For every item of monetization, you need to have written at least fifty words of text. This helps provide value for your readers, who probably don't consider themselves there solely to make you hard cash. Your words are their pay-back for becoming potential customers too.

Amazon

Since the beginning, Amazon has been the place where I make the majority of my money on Wizzley. I know that I'm not alone in that. From conversations on the forums, it seems that everyone does well with this affiliate link.

Before you join us though, you have a couple of big decisions to make.

Which Amazon will you promote? There are several different versions and they do not interact. When I began I was using the UK version. I was strongly advised to switch to the US instead. The country is much bigger, so there's a better chance of attracting readers who want to buy something. The only realistic options on Wizzley are Amazons Canada, UK and US. You have to write in English on the site, and you want to match your language with the Amazon site. If you are selling to the USA, then your articles should be written in American English. Otherwise all of your paying customers are going to think that you can't spell.

Are you going to monetize your Amazon modules through the site directly or VigLink? There is the option of either on Wizzley. Until you are regularly selling well over 100 items per month, the VigLink option is actually better. You will earn 6.8% commission through that company. Amazon starts at 4% and slowly works its way up, depending upon volume of sales.

Google Adsense or Chitika

You may only choose one of these, so it is well to have all of the pros and cons before you.

The received wisdom, from just about everyone, is that Adsense is the more lucrative. You are unlikely to get anyone advising that you choose Chitika over the biggest advertising presence on the internet. Wizzley is optimized for Google Adsense too. You will get three times the adverts on your page with that option, than you would with the other.

No contest and time to move on? Not quite. I'm with Chitika. And I'm going to leave my referral link here, just on the slim off-chance that you decide to opt for that company: https://chitika.com/publishers/apply.php?refid=joharrington

The only two things that Google Adsense has going for it are those things already mentioned. The potential to run foul of the company is both easy and permanent. To even understand what you can and cannot do is difficult. The main terms and conditions document is written in legal language. Their rules and regulations are dotted over several different web-pages. Some aspects contradict themselves. You do not even have to have done anything wrong to have your account closed. Being 'at risk' of wrong-doing is enough. Google do not need to supply any evidence, nor even a hint of what caused you to be kicked out into the cold.

Any outstanding payments will be instantly withdrawn. Cheques in the post will be cancelled, even, in some nightmarish reports, those already cashed into the bank. People have been left with charges to pay over that behavior.

You may ask how Google can get away with it. Their legal team is bigger and better than any that you would be able to afford. One man did bite the bullet and prosecuted them for money due to him. He won his case and half of the internet held their breath waiting for the megalith to fall; and a massive run on others following suit. Google appealed and the judge reversed the initial ruling against it. The rationale was that the company contributes too much towards the US economy. It is currently too big to fail.

Did I choose not to go with Google for ethical reasons? No. I didn't know any of this at the time. I wrote a blog about the riots happening in my city. Google cancelled my Adsense account. I was informed on the forums, by fellow users speculating, that the two were probably related. Others looking into this after the event have further speculated that maybe a visitor decided to nerf my account for a laugh. It would only take one person to go on a clicking spree of the advertizements to get me banned as a bad risk.

I was informed that not only myself, but no member of my immediate family, will ever be able to apply for Google Adsense. This decision is irreversible and permanent. I still have no idea what I did. I have never been able to speak with a real human being.

On the other hand, Chitika's support staff are extremely friendly and definitely flesh and blood. The bottom line may be much lower, but you do not have the paranoia nor the restrictions on what you can or can't write about. I don't think that I would want to return to Adsense now. I know too much about the dark side of Google and I prefer the lower wages than to support them.

You may sign up for Chitika solely on the basis of your Wizzley articles. For Google Adsense, you will need to first gain a publisher's ID from your own website or blog. This can then be used for Wizzley too.

Zazzle

Zazzle is so handy! There's an array of unusual products on just about every subject under the sun. You could add them for the referral commission, or you could add to them for the royalties. If the latter, then your articles serve as promotional avenues too.

Many Wizzley writers began with an affiliate link, then moved on to actually producing their own items for their stores. While creating another revenue stream, it also helps when you are struggling to monetize an article. Can't find anything precisely relevant in any of your affiliate stores? Make something! So much is laid out for you, that even unartistic people like myself can come up with a great looking product.

For example, I wrote a couple of Wizzley articles about my experiences as a partially deaf woman. I am completely deaf in my right ear, which means that I have no concept of direction of sound amongst other things.

Those articles were largely information pieces. If I'm honest, I mostly wrote them as somewhere to point towards, when new internet friends ask what it's like to be deaf. It's proven to be popular with other single-sided deaf people too, if the traffic and comments are anything to go by.

But such things are difficult to monetize. I trawled through all of the usual sites looking for anything relevant. In the end, I gave up and turned to the Zazzle product creation page. I played very nicely there, choosing fonts and color schemes in order to make badges. They included slogans like, 'I'm not talking too loudly. You're listening with too many ears' and 'Nope, I still can't distinguish your voice from the television'. They struck a chord with the very people reading my Wizzley articles. I've sold plenty of them!

If you do decide to open a Zazzle shop, as well as signing up for the affiliation, then mention it on the Wizzley forum. There's a wealth of experience there and people willing to give you advice on it.

AllPosters

I know of several Wizzley authors who have done well with AllPosters. Unfortunately I'm not one of them. You really shouldn't listen to what I have to say at all about this one!

That said, I do know the theory. AllPosters, as the name suggests, is all about posters. The images that they supply range from pop culture slogans through to fine art, visiting photography and historic reproductions along the way. They are perfect for splashing a bit of color into your pages, and for breaking up huge walls of text. It's a way of monetizing even the pictures that you're adding to brighten up your Wizzles.

Because they're primarily used in those ways, the AllPosters modules do not require fifty words written per product placed. You could technically smother your page in posters, then write a mere 400 words (the minimum allowed for a Wizzley article to publish) and see it go through. I wouldn't recommend it though. That kind of behavior is bound to elicit a stern message from the Wizzley moderation team!

VigLink (and eBay)

Wizzley has a site wide deal with VigLink, which will monetize all of those links not covered by the above vendors. Many authors choose to concentrate only on this form of monetization, because of the sheer choice on offer. However, Wizzley do not have a bespoke module for it. You will need to insert URLs into a text or link module instead.

It is via VigLink that all of those eBay modules earn you hard cash. This is both wonderful and frustrating. It's great that it exists at all, but eBay will only pay for converted clicks. This isn't as a commission percentage of the purchased item, but as a standard couple of cents per click. Nevertheless, all of those pennies add up, so eBay modules are still worth it. As my old mother used to say - look after the pennies and the pounds will look after themselves.

The real value in VigLink is in the thousands of other on-line vendors at your disposal. The site has a search function for you to peruse all of the stores available for your monetizing. They include some extremely big names, like Barnes and Noble, Target and Macy's. It's worth shopping around for products to place. For example, Amazon will offer Halloween Costumes at 6.8% commission, if monetized through VigLink. But you could add in precisely the same costume, also monetized through

VigLink, at 15% commission, if you used Wholesale Halloween Costumes.

However, some caution should also be taken. Vendors sign up with VigLink all of the time, but some also leave. You might have a great money-making opportunity, which suddenly falters, because your links are no longer part of the deal. This can render it a lot of hassle to maintain.

You can check what vendors are available by signing into VigLink, clicking on the Tools tab, then hunting through Merchant Explorer.

In the Beginning...

Now you're through the door, all set up and you've introduced yourself on the forum, it's time to get writing.

One thing that you should know before you settle down - your first five Wizzles (articles on Wizzley) will be moderated. This is just a precaution. Right now, the Wizzley team doesn't know if you're the Spammer from Hell or the next J.K. Rowling. They are naturally hoping for the latter.

In real terms, this means that your sparkly new articles won't turn up in a search engine, until someone backstage has clicked a button. Most people pass through this period without even knowing that they are being evaluated. (Because they didn't read the TOS.) Your writing will still be live. You'll be able to post a link to your mother and everyone in your social networking channels, but Google, Bing et al will have to wait a bit.

The only time you will know something about it is if your work doesn't pass muster for whatever reason. It might be that you've written about a subject on the Wizzley Not list, or your grammar and spelling isn't good; or simply that you're not cut out to be a writer. If that's the case, then I'm sorry. But you know about Zazzle now! Can you create art?

After the first five Wizzles, with no problems at all, then everything you publish from now on will automatically go live onto the search engines; and you're well on your way.

So what should you write now? Where should this tale begin? I have three recommendations, though you are perfectly at liberty to go your own way, with me cheerleading right behind you.

a. My first is that you just write. Don't sit back evaluating whether you're good enough, we're good enough, the world's good enough. Nothing ever gets written that way. Assume that everyone and everything is perfect and click on that 'create a page' button.

b. My second is that you have fun. It's going to take you three times as long to write this initial Wizzle, because you will be distracted by finding out what all of the buttons do. Click them! Explore! This is your new sandbox and this is how you deduce the stuff useful to you!

c. My third is that you write a Wizzography as your first article. This ticks a lot of boxes and it's a good one to use for playing/exploring purposes.

What is a Wizzography?

A Wizzography is whatever you want it to be. Even the most cursory glance into that category will reveal a whole potpourri of innovative ways of creating one. Some use it as a biography (as I did); others to tell a specific story about their lives or passions. It's been produced as a kind of index to some galleries. Or to set out dreams and aspirations. This is your place to go wild, so do as you will.

Do note though that your Wizzography is 'no follow' by default, nor will it ever turn up in SERPs. This is where everyone backlinks their internet empire into spam proportions, so we don't need that category bringing the whole site's ranking down.

I consider this a great place to begin because you already know your own story. You aren't burdened by having to research anything nor look for topics to appear passionate about. You can simply write away, in the sure knowledge that it will be right. This frees you up to investigate all of the Wizzley modules and other buttons without losing track of what you were going to write.

However, there are also two more good reasons to complete one of these. The first is that it acts as an extended profile. Those people intrigued by your mini-biography may click on this to find out more. Impress them enough and you may have just found your first returning readers. If they then follow you, they'll receive an e-mail alert whenever you publish an article on Wizzley. Therefore, it's worth bearing in mind the impression that you want to convey, while writing your Wizzography; and what you believe will convince people to follow you.

The second major reason why you should complete a Wizzography is that it fits into your profile header. Your author rank is made up of various contributing factors, but one of those is a completed profile.

In the next chapter, I'll walk you through how to create a page on Wizzley. But I really do recommend that, for your first one, you skip all that I have to say. Just make it yourself and enjoy the process of discovery.

Understanding the Author Rank

Every new writer on Wizzley begins at 0%. The figure at the end of the first paragraph of your profile will inform you what it becomes after that. The highest is obviously 100%, which is what you ideally want to achieve.

I've mentioned before that Wizzley is built to be optimized for search engines and readers. The ranking system is good for both. It is believed that companies like Google love author rankings. It saves them having to make a judgment call in the earliest moments of deciding where to lodge your link in their pages. After a while, it'll have its own data to go on. That said, it might just be an internet rumour, as Google does keep its criteria close to its digital chest and us mere mortals can only guess.

As for potential readers, it stands to reason that an author with a high rank will appear a better choice for a random read, than one with a low rank.

Those with an author rank over 90% gain another benefit too. On the Wizzley home page, their new articles are automatically linked from a feed in the header. Most of my first readers are from Wizzley. My statistics tell me that. I know that it's from that article feed, as that's the only place where the community would be able to spot them being published. I doubt that they all sit there all day refreshing my profile gallery on the off-chance that I just wrote something new.

On the top toolbar of every Wizzley page is a link labelled 'Authors'. Click on that and you'll find every Wizzley author listed according to prowess. This doubles as an introduction to the calibre of writers on the site, so naturally it's arranged so that the better authors are first, then on through all of the rest. Your actual position is determined by an algorithm (hence it's not at all worth bribing the administrators to push you up a few pages).

First are those with many Editor's Choice Awards, through to those with fewer. You can tell those with three or more, as they have a rosette beside their name.

After the award-winners are out of the way, it all comes down to your author rank. We pass through all of those at 100%, ordered as to how recently they posted an article; then on to those at 99% and so on.

This section is another potential source of readers. The closer that you are to the front page, the more likely they will read your fantastic mini-profile information and come to check you out.

Whether you worry too much about your author rank or not is your concern. It does provide a couple of nice, in-house publicity points for your articles and gallery; but the operative word there is 'in-house'. There are Wizzley authors who maintain that it's fundamentally worthless and they're not going to bother achieving a decent rank. Nor have they got one.

Personally, if mine should ever fall below 100%, then I'd be taking immediate steps to nudge it back up again. Fortunately that has never been an issue.

How to Boost your Author Rank

Once you know how your author rank is calculated by the algorithm, then the ways to boost it become obvious. These are the three factors contributing to your final tally:

1. The completeness of your profile information. If you've been following this guide so far, then you've done all that. Allow yourself a moment of accomplishment and a hearty pat on the back.
2. The number of articles published and...
3. ... their quality based upon page rank.

In short, fill in all that you can on your profile, then write often and write well. The author rank will just fall into line without you paying it any heed.

Please note that the author rank is very robust and quite fair. It's not the case that if you went away on holiday for a week, you'd come back to find it at 1%. As long as those page ranks remain high, then your author rank is bound to be too. People will still be reading while you're away.

Understanding your Page Rank

Every article that you publish on Wizzley will enter cyber-space with a rank of 47%. It used to be 50% but it recently dropped down. All being well, it has the potential to climb to 100% in seven days.

Once it does that, it will appear on the Wizzley home page under the heading 'Popular'. That gives it a nice publicity boost. No member of the Wizzley team puts it there. It's again dependent upon an algorithm; and Wizzley's author geeks have hours of fun trying to determine precisely where that algorithm's tipping points lie!

How to Boost your Page Rank

The information about what feeds the page rank is readily available. It's again three factors:

   a. The number of Wizzley likes (the thumbs up icon at the foot of every article).
   b. The amount of readers (determined by internet traffic) and comments that your article receives.
   c. The content and uniqueness of the article.

Every one of my articles has reached 100%. They may slowly fall later on, only to rise back up again in a few months, but that initial interest raised them to 100%. I've always encouraged friends and family to comment on my work. I've personally thanked them, when they've forwarded links to their social networking circles. I respond to every single comment left. All who interact with your Wizzley article - voting in polls, debating on the duel modules, commenting at the end of the article, liking it, Tweeting it, Facebooking it and all the rest - are helping you raise that page rank percentage. You should be grateful that they came to help you.

Wizzley Nots: What You May Not Write About on Wizzley

You can't write about everything that you may want to on Wizzley. This is to cut down on the most common 'spam' subjects, but some are also to comply with the rules of Google Adsense. It's best to approach this list with some common sense. If there's an article that you want to write about, which looks like it may be rejected as a Wizzley Not, then ask about it. Some things are permissible. For example, you can't write an article instructing people how to hack a computer. But you can write a review of *Ghost in the Wires*. The latter is the autobiography of a hacker, not instructions. It's allowed on Wizzley.

- Pharmaceuticals/drugs – reviews and recommendations of drugs and pills.
- Weight loss and diet pills (or supplements) or reviews of e-books on diet related products/services including Acai Berry.
- Link exchanges, traffic exchanges, pay-to-read, banner ad farms, MLM, network marketing, pay per click schemes and the like, together with affiliate programs that have a poor reputation on the Internet.
- "Medical/Alternative Cures" for the like of PMS, yeast infections, acne, PE, snoring, hair loss, breast augmentations, asthma, insomnia, etc. or cosmetic surgery services.

- Help with love life, flirting, sex life, seducing others, managing your "ex".
- Reviews or promotion of (including linking to) dating sites or adult liaison sites.
- Anything to do with gambling, lotteries, poker, etc.
- Sites for downloading/copying movies, music, games, software, ringtones or TV shows.
- Credit card debt, promoting credit card companies, cash gifting, loan company ads, mortgage reduction, Forex, currency or minerals trading, futures, etc. or any topic that offers unrealistic hope for quick debt reduction or fast income generation.
- Copying and sharing video games, including illegal downloads.
- Involving or inciting hate, discrimination, violence or injury (incl. bloody, graphic images).
- Stuff that would be considered R-, X-rated and porn.
- Lyrics – unless you own the copyright or are providing extended commentary on the lyrics of a song.
- Google's trademarked terms in the site's URL.
- Illegal or unethical activities, such as spying, drug use, hacking, cracking, warez, breaching copyright, deception through free games and tv, generating artificial profiles, utilizing black hat marketing systems, etc.
- Activities that could be harmful to health, such as encouraging readers to induce a miscarriage, become anorexic or engage in unsafe practices.

- Sales of beer, hard alcohol, tobacco or tobacco-related products (incl. cigars, cigarettes, e-cigarettes, chewing tobacco, or rolling papers).
- Sales of weapons, ammunition, gun parts, hardware, pistols, rifles, BB guns, sporting guns, air guns, blow guns, stun guns, explosives, and fireworks.
- Sales of products that are replicas or imitations of designer or other goods.
- Sales or distribution of coursework or student essays.

Creating a Page on Wizzley

In the top right-hand corner is the most important link of all on Wizzley. It says 'create page' and this is how you build up your article portfolio on this site. Clicking it will take you to a gateway page, then into the editing suite. It's a lot of fun producing a Wizzley page, with lots of room for creativity and plenty of tools to play with. Nothing goes live until you press 'publish page'. Until then, it can sit in your draft folder for an hour or forever, allowing you to tinker until it's perfect.

Unless you're like me, of course. Then it's write it and get it out. I've never been good at achieving perfection.

Gateway: Create a Page

This area is very self-explanatory, but I'll go through it anyway. The first section is where the article's title is added. For those who know their keywords and SEO, this is usually based upon the most searched words or long-tail phrases for your topic. But it's not the only place where these can go.

One of the hidden wonders of Wizzley is that the URL can be customized. On the right-hand side, just under the title box, is a link in unobtrusive grey font. It reads 'customize URL'.

This is where I tend to put either the second most searched keywords, or those key phrases which couldn't be turned into grammatically correct English, even if you were the best writer alive. URLs don't have to make sense. For example, Best Handbags Known to Humanity would make a wonderful title. Handbags Great would make a good URL.

If you don't alter the URL at all, then it will default

to copying your title. That's fine. It renders it double the search juice!

Summarize Your Article in a Few Words

If your title is the hook that lures people in, then the summary below is the loaded bait to seal the deal. It should be attractive, enticing and explain more about what this article is all about. It will help your prospective readers decide if it's worth the time to check it out.

I really messed this up when I began. It took veteran writer Terri Rexson to take me to one side and have a word, before I saw the error of my ways. I was concentrating so much on being enticing that I was telling nobody anything much. It was practically a form of subterfuge or misdirection. It was like one of those notices which yell, 'SEX!', in big letters, then finish with, 'Now I have your attention, there will be a meeting of the tiddlywinks players' society in the town hall at 7pm tonight. Bring cake.' You'd read the entire flyer wondering if the heading was indicative of the meeting, or if it really was just there to grab your eye.

I took notice after that. If the title doesn't tell you exactly what this Wizzle is about, then the summary will. The best of all writers ensure that both do the job.

Intro - The First Section

Look at any Wizzley article (with Adblock off) and you'll find a short section at the top. When Google Adsense blocks are initiated, then this section forms the text block beside it. It cuts out all of those otherwise ugly white spaces. If the reader has Adblock on, or if Chitika adverts are displayed instead, then the text block will spread across the page. It's flexible like that.

This is where that first section is added into your Wizzley article. Everyone finds their own voice and style with it. I personally keep it short, so it fits the gap perfectly (at 80-100 words). I've done that for purely aesthetic reasons, as I believe it looks better. I also click the 'justify' button underneath for the same reasons.

Others go for many more words, as the resultant wall of text wraps around the Adsense block and draws yet more attention to it. It's worth experimenting to see what you prefer for yourself.

Choosing a Category

There are thirty-two categories on Wizzley at the time of writing. They all split into several sub-categories, which have yet a third tier of sub-categories diving those. It's like an enormous world tree with a vast number of branches. I've been there over a year now, and I'm still occasionally surprised by an unnoticed twig. I'm an enthusiastic gamer, and I only found 'Gifts for Gamers' last week. I've since plonked six articles into it.

Not every category and sub-category is obvious from searching the site. They only exist as potentials until a writer populates one with an article. The only way to explore all that exists is to look through the pull down menus on the gateway page.

The best category for your article is the one which best matches the subject matter. However, there may be multiple choices for that. For example, a Wizzle about a committed gay couple may go in either Culture and Society > Social Issues > Gay Marriage; Family and Relationships > Marriage > Gay Marriage; or Weddings > Wedding Traditions > Same-sex Weddings.

Whatever you decide here doesn't have to be permanent. You can move your article around at will at any time in the future. That way you're able to experiment with the most appropriate placement by looking at real results in the stats later on.

An interesting piece of trivia - the categories and sub-categories were all gleaned from the most popular keywords and key phrases. That's why some repeat themselves in various sections and why some appear a little unusual. Like 'Have a Happy Marriage'.

Then 'Here We Go'!

Main Page: Creating a Wizzle

Now that you're past the gateway, you can begin fitting together your Wizzley article. At the very top there is the information which you have already added via the gateway. This can be edited now, if you wish. It can be edited at any time in the future too. Just click the 'edit' button, in the top right hand corner of the 'Basic Data' module.

As for what lies beneath, the world is your oyster. At least it is if said world only employs the tools amassed at the top of the right-hand sidebar. Only three rules apply to restrain your creativity here. They are:

The content is subject to the rules of Wizzley. No illegal stuff, no gore, if you're happy for your granny to read this, it's probably ok.

Any products placed must be matched by fifty words of text in the rest of the article.

The topmost module cannot be a product placement.

There really is no right or wrong way to design a Wizzley article. Over time, people find their own style and their own voice. Right now, you should be experimenting to see what looks wonderful and works well for your needs.

The only bit of major advice I'd give is to include images. The internet is currently a very visual place and pictures do break up great walls of text. The very first image that you'll need to add is right up the top. This acts as a thumbnail picture in all of the listings. Find something which represents your article in the most relevant and colorful way possible. Those are the ones which stand out.

Adding Modules to a Wizzley Page

Your toolbox is that top right-hand collection of modules. To add one to your page, just click on it.

As your page gets longer, then scroll to the place where you would insert the module. When you click on the toolbox button, it should insert the module precisely where you want it to. If not, there's no problem. Just move your cursor to the top of the inserted module. Hold down your mouse's left-click button and drag the module to where you want it to be. Alternatively, look again to your sidebar. Underneath the modules toolbox, there's a second box with a tab entitled 'Modules'. This allows you to view a kind of blueprint of the whole page. You can drag modules around in there too, then press save at the bottom.

Saving your Progress as you Work

Wizzley is a brilliant site for this. It automatically saves, at regular intervals, all that you do. I was really not used to this. Every site I've written for before Wizzley required a manual save and occasionally even those got lost. This has never happened to me on Wizzley. Closing an edited module will save it. Simple as that.

I was also once in the middle of writing in a text module, when I accidentally kicked the power button on my PC's tower. The whole computer switched off. Sod's Law would have it that the thing I was writing just happened to be heavily researched. I dreaded having to do all of that again. I hadn't closed the module mid-writing either, so I knew that it wouldn't be saved. But it was. Even an aggressive close down like that had triggered Wizzley's hyper-sensitive 'save all' algorithm. I was staring at every word that I'd written, including half of the word that I was attempting to type when I kicked the tower!

The Modules

'A page consists of various modules that can be added from the list at the top right, in edit mode. You can change their position or size by dragging them with the mouse, or clicking on the arrow symbols. Try different possibilities - you cannot do anything wrong.'
- Wizzley's own advice.

I'm going to take you on an exploration of the modules in your toolbox. They are not ordered here as they are in Wizzley, but grouped together according to type. Understanding the aim of some of these modules can give you the edge, when making your Wizzle stand out amidst all of the rest.

The Content Modules

Everything in the 'add module' section is content, but some are specifically for items and words of interest. These are what you give back to your readers in exchange for them taking the time to peruse your page. If your main aim is to make a living, then this bit has to be right in order to attract potential buyers. They won't click on your products, unless they have a good reason to. These modules provide that reason.

Flickr

The word on the street right now is that images rule the internet. Sites like Pinterest, which are fundamentally massive picture galleries, have risen to the top of the pantheon of social networking sites. I've also heard Pinterest unkindly (and inaccurately) described as Reddit for girls. The stereotypical idea being that women prefer a visual array, while men would rather have walls of text. I've found no study whatsoever to back up this assertion, but if it's true then it has implications for us on Wizzley. According to Alexa (which is also fundamentally flawed), the majority of Wizzley's readership is female.

Sometimes half truths grasped are the only clues you have to go on. I thought I'd leave it out there anyway.

The Flickr module is one way of inserting images into your Wizzley article. This is a great place to add whole photo galleries, which your readers can flick through. Either add a specific URL or let the site search for images for you.

Feed

Anything with an RSS link can be inserted into here. I've used it to ensure up to the minute news streams from Google News, as well as adding Twitter feeds. The useful thing here is that it keeps your article current. You can use the article itself as an introduction, while the feed makes it as fresh as if it was written yesterday.

Images

If you have a large picture to display, then I recommend that you use this module, rather than inserting the image into a text module. You will be able to make it fit the entire width of the page, which will help draw attention to it. There's also the capacity to add a title and sub-title.

However, if you're looking for a big, static image to break up walls of text, then it may be worth considering AllPosters instead. It has a huge collection of images, which you can use (in an AllPosters module) without having to hunt around for copyright permissions. There's also a chance of selling the image, thus earning commission.

Link List

I've known writers who wouldn't touch this module with a barge-pole. The whole point of it is to direct readers away from your page. It may not even be to a website which makes you money!

I do use it. My ethos is that the reader is actually the important person here. I can write all that I like, but if they're not reading, then it's all just so much dust in cyberspace. I want my Wizzley articles to be informative, interesting and useful. If someone is writing elsewhere on the internet in a way which enriches what you're saying, then send your readers to them too. Wizzley isn't daft.

Link lists open pages in another tab or window, so your original article is still there, awaiting the return of your readers. They will now be even more satisfied that they came to the right place.

It's so easy in this game to think that you're the center of the universe. Your readers must come, must buy or be damned! Wrong. They come because you make it worth their while. Link lists are just one trick in your writer's arsenal to ensure that is the case.

Besides, you can use this for monetized links. This is a great place in which to shove all of those URLs from VigLink.

Map

If you are writing about a specific place, then it's a nice idea to point to that on a map. Wizzley uses Google Maps to do this, which opens up street-view as well. The map defaults to the USA, but it can be dragged to anywhere else in the world.

By typing in the box, then adding a pin, you can place your reader exactly where they need to look. Multiple pins may be placed.

It may be that in the future this module is opened out to Chitika Maps too. That would be a great blessing, as those maps can be monetized!

Recipe

Sharing recipes can be an extremely lucrative venture for an on-line writer. ChefKeem, one of the co-founders of Wizzley, made his name this way. He knew what he was talking about, as he is a chef in the real world too! In context, it's hardly surprising that Wizzley ended up with its own module to make life easier for recipe writers.

The beautiful thing here is that the module asks for all of the necessary data - ingredients, time to cook, pictures etc - then formats it all for you. You never see anything like this in the History section, I can tell you. Mind you, it wouldn't exactly be useful over there.

Text

This is the main module of all, hence it's number one in your tool-box choices. You could get away with a Wizzley page which only ever utilized this module, though it would look very bland and probably not prove very lucrative.

You have an array of icons along the top of the text box. This can help format your text module in a way which looks good to you. It's worth exploring what all of these buttons do, as they can be very effective tools. From left to right, they are:

HTML. By clicking this, you get to see the coding behind your text module. For those proficient in HTML, then this is real play-time. You can add tags which aren't automatically available to everyone else. However, the Wizzley team has an approved list of tags, so you might not be able to do everything. If you really want something added to that list, then contacting Simon is the way to go.

That can be done privately or via the Wizzley forum. I tend to use this not for formatting per se, but to correct a common issue with text modules. As you write, extra spaces may be created at the bottom. By entering the HTML section, you realise this is because the <p> tags are amassing at the bottom. Delete them and all is well again.

Undo and Redo. If you've accidentally added or deleted something that you didn't want to, then these are the buttons to use to correct it.

Spell Checker. This is the ABC button with a tick beside it. It's automatically set to default, which allows your words to be spell checked as you go along. At the moment, it's not actually possible to stop that, so this is a kind of redundant button!

Formatting Keys. The next quartet relates to ways to display your font. B = Bold; I = Italics; and strikethrough will cross out words, ~~like this~~. The final button removes formatting. You may have copied something from a website, which has deposited a load of dodgy tags all over your text module. If you highlight the words copied again, then click that button, it'll strip the formatting from it.

Subscript and **Superscript**. These two buttons

allow you to display smaller font, which lies slightly ^{higher} or _{lower} than the main text. This may be useful for footnotes.

Font Display. This doesn't change the actual script, but that's fine. If we went too wild here, Wizzley would lose its uniformity and look rubbish. Instead you get a choice of three formatting modes for font. The default position is 'paragraph'. That's just straight display. The second is 'module title', which apes the look of all your titles on the page. The third is 'module subtitle', which copies the formatting for, well, module subtitles. I've never quite seen the point in using either!

Text alignment. The next four buttons align all highlighted text. You get the choice between right align, center, left align and justify.

Bullet points. If you have a list of items in your text module, then it might be an idea to separate them with bullet points or numbers. That can be done easily here. Either type your list, highlight it, then click one of these buttons, or else click the button first. Each time you press enter, it will automatically give you a bullet point to go on with.

Insert image. This is the third and final way of including a picture on your page. This embeds an image into the text module itself, aligning it to the left and resizing it, so it fits across half of the module space. I tend to head all of my full-sized text modules with an image. It breaks up the text and looks attractive.

Hyperlink and **Remove Hyperlink**. Here's where you link to another website (or elsewhere on Wizzley), or, if you've done it wrong, where you break said URL link. Just highlight the words to be linked, then click the button with a chain on it. You will be given a pop up box in which to insert your URL.

Once you start writing in your text module, there will be a final element on that top toolbar - your word count. That pertains to that module only. In order to publish any article on Wizzley, you need to have written at least 400 words across the whole page. To insert a product, you need to have 50 words written. This word count helps you keep your tally.

YouTube

Inserting YouTube videos will not only break up the text, but it may help illustrate a point which you are trying to make. For example, when I review movies, I also include a trailer taken from YouTube. It gives your readers a visual idea of what you're discussing here. If you're writing about a certain gadget, then videos can show that gadget in action.

It's all part of the current SEO advice, which is to employ a range of media on your page. It should also be noted that Google owns YouTube. It could well be good for Google search engine ratings to have this module employed effectively on your page.

The Interactive Modules

Gone are the days when readers passively peruse your articles, enjoying being told things, then going away. The prevailing wisdom in SEO circles is that your articles must be active affairs. Your readers want to participate in some way. These modules help to give them something to do, while they're reading your article.

Duel

Get a debate going! If you've written about something controversial, or merely with a choice, then the duel module opens up the floor for other opinions. Ask a question, fill in the fields with open-ended yay or nay responses, then let your readers pick their sides.

Poll

A poll is the quickest activity going. Your reader only has to click an option and their vote is registered. It's activity on the go, but at least they go to participate. This is better for multiple choice responses, where a polarised, two-horse debate isn't as appropriate.

The Formatting Modules

These modules are mostly about making the page look good for your readers, or else to direct them where they may wish to go.

Article List

It's good practice to link to other Wizzley articles and this is the module to help you do that. This is useful to you, as it helps cut down your bounce rate. It's very useful to your readers. It points them in the direction of other articles that they may enjoy.
The biggest rule of thumb here, on article selection, should be what's good for your reader. Highlight other articles which match the topic of the one that they're reading. Let it enhance your article, not detract from it. This means that you may well be linking to articles which you didn't write.
However, we're all human. 90% of the Wizzley articles linked via the article list promote other work by the same author. That's good too, as long as it really is relevant. It keeps the readers (and potential buyers) with you. But they will also soon get really tired of you, if

you're merely trying to herd them into disparate buying opportunities. What would you like to see here, if you were reading it?

Contents

The contents module helps your readers find things quickly on your page. I tend to put it at the very top. I've occasionally followed the lead of other Wizzley authors, who also include it at the bottom. This means that those finishing your article can swiftly return to something that they want to view again. There are obvious advantages here for sales articles. Your potential buyer has looked at all on offer, now they want to home in on their favored item. Happy days and hopefully much commission too.

Space

As the name implies, this creates a space wherever you place it. It defaults at 5 pixels deep, but you can alter that. I tend to go for 1 pixel, which is the smallest that it can be.
This is most useful when you have a group of half-modules stacked on top of each other. They will rearrange themselves any old way, if you let them. By inserting a space module, you can keep the formatting. While this doesn't matter a great deal when it's viewed on a PC, it does help enormously for the mobile version. This is the way that a growing number of readers are perusing your article, so it's worth making it all look lovely for them.

The Sales Modules

This is where the money is! They may be the most important modules for you, if you wish to make a living by writing for Wizzley. They can also be used to make a page look pretty and break up walls of text. They will all be monetized by VigLink, unless you have your own referral code added into your overall Wizzley settings.

AllPosters

Alone of all the Wizzley product modules, you don't need to write 50 words to facilitate a product placed in here. AllPosters are great for adding general images with a chance of making some profit too.

You have the choice between searching for a subject or adding in the code for an actual poster. To find that code, look beside the picture's title on the AllPosters website. You will see 'Item #:' then some numbers. It's the numbers which you want to add to the 'product number' field. That can be found in the Wizzley AllPoster module, in the second tab.

Amazon

Amazon is one of the biggest earners on Wizzley. You have a variety of ways to find and display products in this module. If you wish to add in a specific product, then look for the ASIN code under each item on Amazon's own website. You usually have to scroll down. It's in the information just above the comment section.

eBay

There is no way to add in your own eBay affiliate code. You have to go through VigLink for this one. It's also not worth highlighting specific products, as this is an auction site. Those products will disappear, when someone buys them.

It's better to search for a subject and let the products update on a real time basis.

Zazzle

You can again search for products, or you can add in items of your choice. To do the latter, scroll right to the bottom of the Zazzle page. Under 'product details' you will see an ID number. That's the one which you need to copy and paste into the Wizzley module.

Is Wizzley a Content Farm?

To the casual observer, Wizzley exists along the same lines as the big names in the genre - Squidoo, Hubpages, Suite101 and all of the rest. The terminally disparaging call them content farms and sneer endlessly about the State of the Internet. Like it was ever picket fences and neat little boxes. When no-one listened the first time, the peanut gallery trolls repeated it, over and over again, until sheer dint of repetition saw some of the mud sticking. Reputations and livelihoods get lost in such cruel games. Years of hard work disappear in the blink of an eye. Especially when Google's spokesperson, in singling out the CEO of one of the sites, echoed the 'content farm' slur, like a megaphone announcement from God.

The internet will always have trolls. People with power will always slip up and say things that they shouldn't. But current affairs and history are always written by the winners; and they choose the words to use.

Wizzley is not a content farm.

A content farm, to my mind, is an operation where keyword stuffed paragraphs are rattled off for cents; where endless lines of links take the place of actual creativity. And in the latter, I do exclude the likes of Reddit, where the titles themselves are fonts of originality. Content farms produce text that is soul-destroying to write and tedious, bordering upon impossible to read. It serves to fill the spaces between adverts, in order to game the search engine algorithms into top rankings. It's all about the money. Not about the content, despite the name.

It's the internet equivalent of someone sticking a flashing, neon light billboard in between the *Mona Lisa* and Van Gogh's *Starry Night*. It might catch everyone's attention, but that doesn't mean that it's good; and that is the perennial problem of the search engine companies - filtering out the dross, so we just get the art, in a cyber-space which (quite rightly) refuses to be regulated. Hence sledgehammer approaches like Panda and Penguin, Google's latest atom bombs into the online writing world. They were supposed to scorch the content farms; but too many other websites got caught in the firestorm.

Wizzley did not. It avoided the initial direct hits by virtue of not being around. It's bimbled blithely through the aftershocks by having been forged in the hard lessons which followed Panda. While older, more established online writing platforms struggled to reverse their mammoth bulk onto a course more amenable to Google, Wizzley had no need. It was able to launch already poised on the starting line of the right track. It's darted ahead ever since.

But if Wizzley, as an internet magazine, is new to the field, then the team behind it is not. Like elder statesmen and women, they have done their years in the ranks of writers. They were there when the big name sites were start-ups; and they witnessed every twist in the journey unto now. They watched the heady, early rise of the industry; the hey-day; and the influx of people after easy money. They saw the saturation point of black hat SEO practices come and build beyond its limits, until it had to crash and burn. They stood amidst the incriminations, the backlash, the tears and the panic. They experienced the knee-jerk wrong turns of complacent CEOs, shocked into reaction in attempts to stabilize their tottering business strategies.

Achim, Anne, Simon, Hans and Ron saw these not as generals, but as soldiers in the war-zone of an online writing industry finding its place in the cyberworld. And they took notes. And they carried that wealth of experience and knowledge into a fresh-faced website, with an entirely clean slate.

All that ultimately worked, they built into Wizzley from the beginning. All that turned out to be toxic was guarded against in the TOS. It's the healthy, green shoot, the fresh ray of hope, in a post-Panda-apocalyptic internet writing world. Its future is already bright. Its caretakers put in the effort and hours to make certain that it stays that way.

And the authors, they write. Encouraged by a community made up of fellow writers from top to bottom, buoyed by the sense that we're all in this together; and that it will be great. You can get an education here, freely given and happily received; veterans reaching out to novices and newcomers bringing fresh ideas and a marked lack of bitterness. Too many disappointments rained down before, the latter is needed more than most will admit.

Wizzley is a new site, with firm foundations and a steady rate of growth. Its community is formed in friendliness, where every voice is heard, insights abound and the management keep everyone informed. The articles pouring into its categories are kept at a high level of quality, which some might call too strict and others merely applaud. Those not making the grade are handed back with guidance, in the hope that they can be brought up to scratch, and maintained at that quality.

In the paper world, that would be termed an editorial standard, so it is online too. Wizzley is a magazine, and an increasingly respected one at that. It is going to be huge!

The Future for Wizzley

Without a crystal ball, it's impossible to guarantee the future of any site. Online writing is not a business built on certainties anyway. Websites fall, or are catapulated to greatness, seemingly at the fickle whim of The Internet, unless a Google algorithm gave them a push. Where Wizzley will fit into the grand cyber scheme of things can only ever be a matter for speculation. However, we can look to its past and present for pointers towards its future.

The most important thing to note is that Wizzley is currently a very young site. It is only two years old in 2013. For those writing there now, this is a wonderful boon. It means that all of the best subjects have not yet been taken. There are whole categories and sub-categories awaiting articles to populate them. A savvy internet writer can dance across them, with all of the abandon of a gleeful child contemplating a field of virgin snow. This is the place to establish your authority in a niche; and it's growing all of the time.

Each day more authors register their accounts. They range from the newcomers here to earn, while they learn their trade, through to veterans in this game. Some bring with them portfolios of hundreds of articles (each carefully removed and delisted from previous URLs). Some create whole new profiles, never before seen in cyber-space. They all bring with them their own networks of readers, friends, family and casual passers-by. With every moment, Wizzley grows that little bit more. The future is there for the taking.

The great buzz right now comes in that certain and sure knowledge that today's writers are in at the ground floor. As the writing platform matures, then so do our articles. By the time Wizzley truly reaches its potential, then our work will be ready and waiting to reap the full rewards.

I've already seen it begin to happen. When I arrived, on December 16th 2011, Wizzley was a relatively small concern. The forum was full of very friendly people, but the same names recurred. You got the impression that many were there as a favor to the owners. A handful of articles to help found the platform, while their authors were really concentrating their efforts elsewhere. Yet none of them actually left, and eighteen months on many of those earliest authors are focusing their efforts here. Such things speak volumes to me.

During that time, I've watched the pace of incomers accelerate. There were once perhaps two or three new accounts a day. Now it's difficult to keep up with them all. There were times when the same handful of people commanded the front page, because there were so few of us penning popular pages. These days, the mix is far greater. Their topics alternate several times a day. It feels like Wizzley went from a busy village to a thriving town within the course of just a few months; and it's only just begun.

Like any new writer, putting in the effort and needing some quiet reassurance, I've searched the internet looking for clues to Wizzley's potential. I've found plenty of comments from those cynical and jaded individuals declaring Wizzley to be another flash in the pan. I've then watched, as the weeks go by, the same people suddenly turn up as authors themselves. Their instincts are bringing them to our digital doors. I'm glad that I joined long before. It's validation that I made the right decision, and that is sweet.

No-one can say for certain what the future is for Wizzley. But all of the indicators are looking positive. In this business, that's about as good as it gets. I, for one, am staying put and building my Wizzley profile. All of the promise has been fulfilled thus far.

Bonus Material: Tips and Tricks on Wizzley

It's so easy to become overwhelmed. Those who have newly arrived as an online writer have much to learn. Those who have been around for years find themselves with too many writing channels to maintain. When I began writing, I was besieged by well meaning advisors. I loved each and every one of them for their kindness, but it was a lot to take in.

More to the point, I had no way of judging the value of their advice! There were some whose word I took as gospel, until it became clear that they only looked knowledgable to those who knew nothing. There were others whose every word of advice was like a gold nugget. Unfortunately too much of that blinds you in the gleam.

In the end, I gave those who followed me what I dearly wished I'd had for myself. A regular journal of tips and tricks, which chronicled all that I was learning (publicly, so that other veteran writers could leap in, if I was going awry) and how the theory panned out in reality. These articles were (and still are) written after every fifty Wizzles. They all finished with my statistics for the intervening period. Anyone reading could see for themselves whether my strategies were working out. They could pick and choose the things that they were going to nick for themselves.

What follows has all been previously published, as part of the Tips and Tricks series on Wizzley. The only amendments made are triggered by the information no longer being current. Please read these articles in the spirit in which they were originally written, that of a young writer on an epic journey to discover all that Wizzley had to offer, and to pass those discoveries on to my peers.

Tips and Tricks After 50 Pages on Wizzley

- Published on February 6th 2012

The first fifty articles on any site are hard work. Yet that crash course provides insights that soon become second nature. At the beginning, it seems that nothing much happens. A new site, a new career, and a painfully slow building with little reward. The hits bobble along, barely rising, before sinking again. The monetization sheets show rows of zeros.

The majority of on-line writers give up long before they see a return on their hard work; and it is hard work. More than many anticipated. Will you be able to stay the pace? Could you keep yourself motivated unto the other side of oblivion?

How to Start Writing for Wizzley

First you create a page. Write it. Publish it. Rinse. Repeat. Write often, write well.

That is the golden rule for anyone trying to build a reputation or revenue with on-line articles. Beyond SEO and page lay-out, it remains the key to it all. But for those just beginning on Wizzley or anywhere else, it feels like there should be so much more. Hours get lost in the half-formed panic of reading endless articles offering advice on how to make it big. Like this one, in fact. But the rest is refinement. The underlying principle never changes, no matter how the story is told. Write often, write well.

This was the philosophy with which I entered Wizzley. I'm fairly new to this game. Nearly 130 articles on Suite101 helped me learn how to write on-line, but every site is different. Wizzley and Suite101 appear to me like chalk and cheese, but it didn't take long to realize that, beneath their differences, the same advice held true. Write often, write well.

I started writing for Wizzley on December 16th 2011. For three weeks, I struggled to get my daily hits above double figures. The chart trickled along, telling me that people were reading, but not really that many. Not enough for it to register in the monetization. The wise souls talk of giving it time. But hours of research and writing are exhausting. Ploughing on with no guarantee of success takes a serious amount of will-power. Then you hit a mental brick wall.

Writing often and writing well is all good in theory, until you actually have to do it. How do you find the motivation to go on investing the time and talent?

How to Stay Motivated

Give yourself small, manageable and achievable goals.

Regular readers will know that I often write about Runescape. Zezima, a famous player of the game, has hi-scores which are the stuff of legend. He was once asked how he achieved them and his answer applies here too. Zezima said that he gave himself tiny challenges on a daily basis. They were each small enough that he could attain them. They acted as little checkpoints, milestones, moments of real achievement. They gave him enough satisfaction to set the next goal.

In the days of few hits on my articles, I stole his technique. Today's challenge was to invite one more reader to look at my writing. Tomorrow's will be to get 50 hits, instead of 48. The next day, I will strive for three articles in one day!

I didn't lose motivation, because I was too busy wooting over all my little achievements.

How Does Wizzley Actually Work?

I'm not ChefKeem, Simon, Nightowl nor any of the excellent team here. But I have eyes in my head.

Another thing that an inveterate, old gamer like me has picked up from the pixel world is to inspect your area. If you don't, then you could be working away forever without having noticed that the secret lever is just behind that boulder; or that a fire-breathing dragon is about to own you from behind. (For the record, I've searched the entire of Wizzley and there wasn't a single boss monster lurking. Stay calm and carry on writing.)

Understanding how Wizzley works can help you from day one in crafting successful articles. This is, in no small measure, because the whole site has been set up by veteran writers. All the little tricks and tweaks are designed to give pointers to readers and writers alike on the best pages out there.

Take the front page. There are three sets of top seven articles on the site. Visitors get their value here, because they can tell instantly what's brilliant, up-to-date and worth reading. You want to be in that list! Publicity is good!

So how do you get there?

Editor's Choice. The first top seven are those latest articles to be awarded an accolade by the Wizzley team. The only way to be there is to write often and write well. If that fails, then you're doing something wrong, so go and study those that did make the grade. Work out why they're so good, then nick every tip and trick that caught your eye.

Popular. These are the individual articles that have most recently ranked 100% across the site. To be on here, you'll have to work on boosting your article's ranking. We'll come back to this.

Buzzing. These seven articles have got people

talking. If you want to be on this list, then you need to start persuading visitors to leave comments on your page. Invite them to do so by asking their opinion or the answer to a certain question. If readers are returning to Facebook or a forum to discuss it, wade on in there and shepherd them all back onto your Wizzley page.

Just trying to achieve a listing, in any of those three, will mean that you're on the right lines to being a great writer. It practically forces you to be brilliant, to write fantastic content, promote it and answer any comments that come your way. All best practice stuff!

Your Article's Ranking

This needs to be 100%!
Take a close look at the little picture beside any article listed on Wizzley. There are plenty on the front page, topic pages or profiles to inspect. Run your cursor over it and some information will appear, including that article's Wizzley ranking. The highest is 100%; presumably the lowest is 1%. You're aiming for triple figures!

Several factors funnel into that score: the number of hits; comments; Wizzley likes (blue button); and social networking buttons pressed. It's all about providing content that people not only want to read, but tell the world about it too. But it's a moving quantity. If people stop clicking anywhere near that page, then your ranking will fall.

By the same token, even if your article is languishing down in a single figure ranking, it's not game over. You can still recover it enough to take it right to the top.

How to Turn Around a Failing Article Ranking

Every Wizzley page starts at 47%. What happens next, for the rest of your days, is up to you. If your article ranking is starting to fall, then that's your signal to promote it again. Be careful though. No-one in your social networks will love you, if you spam them every day with the same thing.

Better still write something else on a similar topic. You can add a 'more articles like this' kind of link back to the one that's falling, as long as it's relevant. That might generate some more publicity, which will bring visitors to boost your ranking with hits, clicks and comments.

Obviously, this isn't suitable for all things. That clever percentage appears to keep things up-to-date by calculating how recently all the activity occurred on your article. If everyone liked it at Christmas, then it'll be slipping into the 90s by February. That's about right, if your subject matter is Santa Claus. No-one wants to be reading about him come summer.

If your page rank never crept too high to begin with, then a revamp might be in order. Take a good, long look at your content and work out why it's not very popular. Does it answer all that you set out to address? Is it aesthetically pretty? Have you got lots of lovely keywords, but not over-stuffed it?

If you can't find anything wrong, then Wizzley has a whole forum category for article feedback. It's there for you to bring in the experts and let them point out the room for improvement. That might not even be a complete rewrite. Some solutions are surprisingly simple.

I had a page which was inspiringly called Studying History as a Timeline. It wavered around the 60% mark, then tottered and began falling. I co-opted a couple of friends to read it and tell me why it was so bad. They aren't people to refrain from calling me on my rubbish, so when they informed me it was fine, I believed them. The only negative feedback they could muster concerned the extremely boring title.

All I did was rename it. The rank immediately began to climb all the way up to 100%, where it's stayed ever since.

Forming a Writing Strategy on Wizzley

The things I find to write about aren't as random as they may appear.

Wizzley is a relatively new platform in which to select your topics. So many categories, or sub-categories at least, are completely empty of content. Write for it and you're guaranteed a niche front page for a little while to come. In a similar vein, the opposite can be over-subscribed. When there exists a plethora of excellent articles discussing a certain subject, it is difficult to make your own stand out.

Recently half of Wizzley were writing about love and romance, as Valentine's Day is fast approaching. While the articles came thick and fast, I noticed that only one aspect remained untouched. The Anti-Valentine's Day category was almost empty! I went against the grain in writing a couple of articles for it. They are now both in my current top five most popular pages. I stepped away from the madding crowd and it was noticed. There is also a reason why I wrote two.

I've started to think in terms of 'support' articles, based on a snippet of information that I've carried with me since high school. That's when my music teacher finally got the class's attention by explaining how the Top 40 worked. (A note for younger readers. Back in the days when dinosaurs ruled the Earth, we bought vinyl singles from the shops. The most sales led to a ranking in the Top 40 on Radio One. It was the most important thing ever, when I was a teenager.) Mr Smallwood explained that bands always released their next single, while the first was starting to fall down the charts. That way fans got the publicity in waves and the rock-stars remained famous.

If it's good enough for the Beatles and Duran Duran, it's good enough for Wizzley writers. I tend to look at which of my articles the front page has listed, then write a second article on the same subject. When people finish reading the one with all of the publicity, they might check out others in the same category and get to my brand new entry in at number 47!

With this in mind, I'm trying out a cycle of subjects, with the same ones recurring. You can catch me at it, if you look to see what articles of mine are currently on the Wizzley front page. Visit my profile and it's highly likely that my latest page will be on the same topic.

I've also taken the advice of fellow Wizzley writers, in order to understand and improve my writing as I've gone along. This includes Jimmie's encouragement to write a blog series. I have several on the go, which are all in there in my writing cycle. I co-ordinate the backgrounds on them, so you can tell you're in the same set!

On Wizzley, Write Often, Write Well

I can't claim to know it all after less than two months on Wizzley. I haven't even scratched the tip of the iceberg with all of the possibilities that lie beneath. However, those fifty pages have given me the opportunity to learn about the platform, and experiment with some fledgling strategies. It appears to be working well enough so far.

On the day I started, forty-six people read my only article. Fifty-two days later, 458 unique visitors were recorded; and that was when I added my 50th Wizzley article. Nearly 11,000 people have been to peruse my content here.

The monetization channels are starting to notice too. The clicks are registering and the zeros are starting to turn into odd pennies. It's not enough to take off on a world cruise nor buy a Ferrari. It's not even going to get me a cup of tea in a greasy cafe; but it's a start. It tells me that I'm on the right track.

For now, the future is simple. Keep on learning, experimenting and refining my writing strategies, but most of all, write often and write well.

Tips and Tricks After 100 Pages on Wizzley

- Published on March 21st 2012

As a relatively new writer, I'm learning my craft on Wizzley. Every fifty pages I pause, record all of the tips and great advice that I've picked up to date. It serves as a reminder and a journal; but more to the point, it offers a helping hand to those following in my footsteps. These are the things that I wish I'd known, when I started out. Fellow new writers get to leap-frog ahead, learning from my mistakes and running with my successes. Good luck all!

Time is a factor. Not merely the time to research and write all of those articles, but to wait for them to bring readers to you. It's easy to envy those who have been around for a while. Their names are known and the search results find them. But a writing career is like planting a tree. The best time to have begun was twenty-five years ago. The second best time is right now!

Get Involved in the Wizzley Forum

It should be noted that the tips and tricks in this Wizzle are probably much more relevant to new on-line writers than those wonderful veterans.

The latter are able to hit Wizzley running and start monetizing their articles immediately. For the rest of us, the first fifty are largely a site and writing genre learning curve; while the second fifty concern the nitty gritty of revenue streams. The good news here is that those with experience are so very willing to help! Any question in the Wizzley forum is likely to produce a wealth of knowledge and understanding, alongside some very practical advice.

I don't just mean the message board forum, which is always buzzing with such information anyway. I'm an historian, so my mind takes in the original, fuller etymology, which today would be much better rendered as community.

Forum, from the old Roman assembly, primarily meaning 'marketplace'; but also open spaces or public spaces. It's related to the Latin 'foris', which involved going outdoors or outside your own domain.

To get involved in the Wizzley forum is to seek out your fellow authors. Leave comments, likes and all of the other paraphernalia of approval on the articles that you enjoyed. Private message them with constructive criticism or point out typos, if you have anything there to say.

All of this is more than merely being a nice person. It pays dividends in community feeling too. In turn that contributes to Wizzley being a lovely place in which to hang out and write. That has to be a winner, because we're all spending so much time here!

Ask Not What Wizzley Can Do For You, But What You Can Do For Wizzley!

On a personal level, so much of the valuable advice given to me over the past fifty articles has been through private messages. Veteran writers giving a hand up into the higher levels of monetary understanding.
With all of their experience, they 'got' it a lot faster than I did. If I'm made great, then Wizzley is made greater. If Wizzley is so wonderful, then more people visit and the knock-on benefits for all authors are increased.

This was an aspect which was brought home to me while chatting on another forum. A commentator there said, "Why are you writing for Wizzley? I've never heard of it! You should go to Hubpages or somewhere like that instead."

He was reaching for familiarity, as a reader, rather than any real knowledge of the writing sector. I suppressed my shudder, born of reading some of the horror stories, but took a note of the important point in the middle of his comment.

People like brands. People like names that they can trust, which doesn't necessarily mean those with their best interests at heart. It's more likely to refer to labels that are known. Familiarity doesn't really breed contempt. It attracts a lot of traffic instead.

At the same time I was reading that comment on another forum, there was a big push being promoted in the Wizzley forum. This didn't come from the site owners (though they appeared happy enough!), but from those veteran writers.

They were telling us that it was time to get the name of Wizzley out there. Make it familiar and readers will come. Tell your friends; tell your social networking contacts; shout it from the rooftops! Wizzley is wonderful! Wizzley is great! Come and bring your family with you!

With a writing platform as new as ours, the emphasis is not only on pushing your own articles on the world, but promoting your environment too.

Are You the Best Person to be Writing that Wizzle?

It's too common to sit inside your own writing empire, keeping the best keywords to yourself and never venturing out to see how everyone else is doing. It's even more tempting to keep interesting and potentially lucrative topics to yourself, regardless of your ability to write anything half-decent about it.

It seems to me that the sites which suffered worse under Google's infamous Panda algorithm were those stuffed with sub-standard articles. When money considerations over-ride value for your readership, then no-one is a winner. Too much of it can see a website sink under the waves of the SERPs.

Conversely, letting a fellow author write that content raises the bar on the whole of Wizzley. It could inadvertently have side-benefits for yourself.

Let me give you an example from the last few days. As an aforementioned historian, I was looking at the 100th anniversary of the sinking of the Titanic with a view to how that slotted into the context of the century. That's what I do. That's what I have bits of paper declaring me qualified to talk about. What I have no knowledge about whatsoever is art. So when I looked at the most promising keywords and saw that Frank Davis Millet had gone down with the ship, I wavered slightly. The man was a famous artist, could I do justice to an article about him? No, but Mladen could.

One private message later, he had the tip-off and duly produced the Wizzle. The site now had an historian writing about history and an art enthusiast writing about art, both about the same broad, highly relevant topic.

That was undoubtedly great for Wizzley, but the inadvertent benefit for myself very quickly became apparent too. Mladen didn't bother too much about the history of the Titanic, as that wasn't his focus. Instead, he linked to my article. Hurrah! A back-link! But his Wizzle ranked faster than mine, due to all of the wonderful comments that he received. (Remember that this is a man who knows his stuff!) While my history is bubbling away, steadily climbing, his is already attracting a lot of early attention - along with a back-link back to mine.

Incidentally, that does go both ways. My Titanic history includes a back-link to Mladen's art appraisal of Frank Davis Millet. Our articles will continue to support each other's into, well, infinity?

That's just one example amongst several. It happens a lot back-stage at Wizzley. Watching each other's backs leads to a much greater website for all involved; and that certainly places our readers right at the top of our priorities.

Is that a Panda that I can see smiling fondly back at us?

Taking the Time to Implement Good Advice

I was exhausted. This much was apparent in the fact that I burst out crying, when my game wouldn't load. My friends listening over Skype were naturally a little perturbed about this. They were used to me getting a little emotional over the important things in life (like failing in Runescape boss fights), but generally I'm quite calm and laid-back about other quibbles (like battling genocide, mass pollution of land and water and dictatorships). I'm certainly not usually in tears over my writing career!

"Go and get a cup of tea," advised the ever pragmatic Tabt. "Calm down, then come and tell us all about it."

The fact is that with so much excellent advice on Wizzley, the temptation is to apply it all at once. When this involves things which can be retrospectively applied, then that can turn into a big job.

I had just emerged from eight hours' worth of systematically going through every one of my previous articles and changing their language. This followed feedback from the ever helpful Terri Rexson, who had pointed out that my adverts all sold merchandise in American stores, while my articles were all in British English.

In short, those buying were looking at an article which appeared littered with spelling mistakes. Those reading perfect English were met with sales that they couldn't make. Who precisely was I serving here?

I doubt Terri actually meant that I should then spend the rest of my day in a frenzied fit of spell-check fuelled up-dating. It's what I did anyway; and I had over eighty articles at the time.

Unfortunately, this was the second such incident in a month. The earlier one came after great advice from always supportive Humagaia. He'd reviewed my sales techniques (non-existent, relying upon politely unassuming adverts quietly placed, more in hope than expectation that someone would investigate them). He'd then given me some beginner's advice.

He had the measure of me. He actually started his message with the statement that he wasn't going to overwhelm me with tips. He'd start with the most important: Invite people to buy! Actually put it into the affiliate module - buy this! Though also include the reasons why. It all felt way too in your face for my British sensibilities, but he assured me that it was the way forward.

Once I'd assimilated the formula, I set about updating the affiliate modules in all previous Wizzles. It took around two days to do and left me exhausted before I even encountered Terri's advice.

So here is some of my own - listen indeed to those wiser minds around you, and implement their good advice. But do it slowly. Burning out will help no-one in the long run, least of all yourself. It will only lead to tears, when your game won't load later on.

And talking about gaming...

A Little Bit of Chaos in the Heart of Ol' Wizzley

There's me thinking that I'm such a paragon of order and planning...

I remember once sitting, minding my own business, as you do, while all around me people were discussing Dungeons and Dragons. They were fixating themselves upon the alignment charts within it. I must have been a little too quiet for too long, or they'd run out of things to say, because suddenly one friend was loudly declaring, "Of course Jo is Chaotic Good."

"She is not!" Countered a second friend, with absolute certainty. "She's definitely Chaotic Neutral. You've never seen her dox!"

"It's not doxing," I mumbled, barely heeded in the on-going fervent debate, "It's called genealogy." But no-one was listening. They were all having too much fun trying to place me in the Dungeons and Dragons alignment system. This whole discussion went on for a good ten minutes, but one thing was clearly apparent throughout. They were the only two categories on the table. I thought maybe Neutral Good for me, but everyone else laughed en masse. I guessed not then.

Whether good or neutral, my presence appeared to stir up some measure of chaos. So how is that working out for Wizzley then? After 100 articles posted here, my fellow authors have had the chance to find out.

The prolifically talented Humagaia wrote an article about using Twitterfeed to promote your articles.

I tried it out. Got mega-hits for a day. Had my Twitter account suspended.

Humagaia responded with much backstage sympathy and information collecting. Then wrote a warning article about how not to get banned from Twitter while taking his advice.

A month later, Twitter reinstated my account after reviewing it and realizing the suspension had all been a big mistake.

Humagaia must love me to bits!

Then there's generous Sam, who approached me in compassion after realizing how bad I was at monetizing on-line articles. After several hours of helping me, she was suddenly inspired with a side-line business in keyword searches for newcomers! (Bless her and Humagaia both. Their tips earned me my first two sales!) So maybe chaos in the heart of Wizzley isn't too much of a bad thing. Even if someone did stop being my 'fan' after I posted an article criticizing executions using the electric chair. I don't know who it was, but in the immortal words of Billy Bragg, "If you've got a blacklist, I want to be on it."

(And incidentally, have you thought of writing a 'pro death penalty' Wizzle? The Human Rights section really does need a bit of balance, in the midst of all of my 'anti death penalty' articles.)

Write About Your Passions!

There's a prevailing bit of advice, which I've been given time and time and time (repeat until fade) again.
 Yet I still ignore it.   It's not that I think the advice unsound. In fact, it's flashing neon with promise, potential and a long, long precedent. But I can't make it fit me. It's like that scene in West Side Story, when Maria is being told to forget about Tony, as he's no good for her.
She warbles back with an impassioned defence,
I hear your words
And in my head
I know they're smart,
But my heart, Anita,
But my heart!
At least, it's a bit like that. Maybe. Perhaps. (Did I really just liken articles that I want to write about to Maria getting a dodgy boyfriend in a gangland musical?)
 The advice is this - write about things that will sell. More to the point, stop writing about human rights, activism and saving the world. Nobody wants to read about those things over morning coffee nor after a hard day at work!
But my heart, Anita, but my heart!
There are plenty of other topics which are, by all accounts, extremely lucrative for on-line writers. Rule of thumb - if it's on the main display stands of huge shopping mall stores, then write about them. Articles like that sell big

time.

I hear your words and in my head I know they're smart...

After several months of this (across several forums, I'm not just talking Wizzley veterans' advice here), I had to face facts. There were two of those: a) human rights issues will never make me rich (but frankly, it would be wrong if they did!); and b) I will not be able to stop writing about them. We're talking about passion versus business acumen; and I never had much of the latter to start with.

But then something quite remarkable started to happen. After months of those articles sitting there and trickling hits, people started clicking on book links to find out more. I was stunned. This wasn't supposed to happen. Those links were there mostly in the capacity of 'for further information' rather than any hope of me getting commission from the sales.

In fact, some of them were a barely disguised back door route into checking out the websites of activist groups fighting the highlighted human rights abuses. If, for example, you didn't notice that my Amnesty International article was one huge AI fund-raising page, then you missed the primary point. (I could just as easily have answered Page's questions via e-mail.)

I bolted like a startled bunny into the Wizzley forum to point back to the situation with a questioning look. The answer soon came back - they're responding to the sheer passion that I put into my words. There was no 'market' here, so I went right ahead and forged one.

What stories do YOU have to share with the world?

The Final Word on Waiting

Time is a factor, of course it is, but we have all of the time in the world. As long as Wizzley exists, then our articles will be out there making us money long after we're all dead.

The trick is to be patient in the beginning. Sam told me that it can take over three months for your page rank to settle in the SERPs. Countless people have told me that it can take far longer for you to see any return on your hard work.

Any on-line writing platform promises jam tomorrow, which is why we munch on our plain bread today. But the future for Wizzley is looking very good. At the time of writing, I have been here a mere three months, just at the minimum for Sam's observation to kick in for reality.

My readership is steadily growing and the earliest indications of revenue are just being sounded. Two purchases in the past fortnight, after weeks of nothing at all. Wish me luck, as I wish it for us all.

Tips and Tricks After 150 Pages on Wizzley
- Published on June 10th 2012

The learning curve goes on and with it comes some amazing insights. But what will work in the long term? When I began writing on-line, I thought that all you needed to do was open a page and start typing. The readership would come and riches would be made overnight.

It's quite a rude awakening to realize that the real world doesn't work like that.

My on-line writing apprenticeship is being served in the friendly halls of Wizzley. As I explore, discover and learn, I am pausing every fifty pages to share what I know. These articles are both my notes and a bread-crumb trail of useful tidbits for those following on my path. It becomes second nature after a while. Waking up, writing, publishing, praying. Will this be the one to go viral? Will this be the one to pay its way?

The more you post, the more chances you get. Write well and write often is as relevant now as it was before. Meanwhile I watch the hits rising; and the rows of zeros on the balance sheet turn into pennies. All of the important data is going in the right direction. Six months in and 150 articles later, there's enough there to remain encouraged. My little saplings are taking root and growing shoots.

"Are you making much money yet?" Other Wizzley authors ask me, more in expectation than hope. I share their enthusiasm. It's happening. Slowly, gradually, like continents shift, but it's happening.

Sometimes on my journey, I find ways to rush ahead. Little tips and tricks that I will share with you now.

Are You Writing About the Right Things?

By which we should first ask ourselves what do we want from each article?

We all have our moments, our flashpoints of meaning, our ways to write our stuff. Sometimes it's vacuous, scribbling down descriptions of what is merely popular, in the hope of attracting readers. Sometimes it's cathartic, writing our paragraphs to assuage the passion, because not getting it out is inconceivable. And sometimes it rests there in the middle, following interests into articles, because we might as well. I should think that it's obvious, which ones belong to which category, for me and for everyone else.

I'm being constantly told by the veteran writers here that there are two kinds of articles. The first is where the majority of mine are placed. They are information articles, which don't necessarily pay well. They answer questions for readers wishing to learn about something; or they raise awareness.

The great money spinners are in the second category. They tap into people's wish to buy something. Those reading already have their credit cards out, they are just looking for the best item to purchase.

Before you write a word, you need to work out what you want from this Wizzle. If it's money, then glorified advertizements in prose form is the way forward. If it's a lot of readers, then in-depth studies of a particular subject are the way to go.

Owning the Popular Category!

One day last week, every article on the front page of Wizzley was written by me. The first that I knew about it was when Janet21 pointed it out on the Wizzley forum.

She blithely asked, "Should they rename the popular category to Jo Harrington? Every page listed there right now is hers!" It was all followed by a beaming smiley face to show that Janet had pointed this out in good humor.

My jaw dropped. I rushed to the front page and cycled through the articles. There are three lists there. I'd recently received an Editor's Choice, so I was at the top of that one. Lots of people were leaving comments on my Wizzles, so I had three or four in the 'buzzing' list too. But the 'popular' category was filled from top to toe with only my work. It felt like an astounding achievement. It felt embarrassing. I was caught between being ridiculously proud of myself, and wanting to hide under a rock. After all, none of the other Wizzley authors could get a look in, while I was dominating the front page.

Even more remarkable was the fact that I hadn't even been here. I'd been visiting friends near Liverpool for four days.

So how had I done it? In order to get into the popular category, you need to have activity on your article. People have to like it, Tweet links to it, send it to Facebook, Digg, Reddit, StumbleUpon and the rest. Moreover, they have to be leaving comments. Even then, these things take time to rise to the page rank of 100, which would cast it into the popular category. Four days is the least of it, hence we can discount the fact that I hadn't been here.

I believe that three factors lined up to push seven of my articles onto that list at the same time. The first is that I tend to write 'information' type Wizzles. This attracts more readers willing to share or comment. I always respond to comments. It would be rude not to, but it also counts towards your page rank. The second is that I had been working very hard before going away. I'd written at least one Wizzle a day, which placed them all in a position where they could rise to that category one after the other.

But importantly, other people weren't writing so much. This was over a weekend, which is always slow. In my native Britain, it was also the Diamond Jubilee period. People were at events and parties, or were taking advantage of the two national holidays to go on vacation. Between the two facts, there was little competition for my articles to take over.

Writing well and writing often had struck again; but add to that one more tip - write when no-one else is doing the same!

Where Are You Placing That Wizzley Article?

Experimenting with the categories and sub-categories can pay dividends, when you finally get it right.

One of the major aspects of Wizzley that I have been concentrating on recently is the categories. There are hundreds of them to choose between - so have you made the right choice? The beauty of this writing platform being so young is that many of the categories haven't yet been populated with articles. Creating a Wizzle for one of them is like running out over virgin snow. Everyone is going to see your footsteps for some time to come.

Tip number one then is to find sections where no-one has written anything. Then take it over. Just one article there is great for starters. Anyone interested in that subject will only have your Wizzle to read!

There is another bonus in that the parent category takes the topmost article from each of the sub-categories. It determines their position on its front page. For example, the front page of Social Issues appears to list top-ranking articles in the order in which they were written. It doesn't, but the difference is one of omission. It actually takes the top four from each sub-category. The most recent is at the top.

Right near to the bottom is an article which I wrote

about the Mole People back in March. There have been pages which attained top ranking in the meantime, but they've been superseded by others in their sub-category.

The Mole People article has retained its position because no-one's written anything to beat it in the Homelessness section. If you want an article to remain in a prominent position in the parent category, then consider placing it in an under-used sub-category yourself.

However, this isn't always the best course of action. Let me demonstrate with another of my articles.

Finding a Place for the Archie Gay Marriage Controversy

There are two likely sub-categories - gay marriage or gay marriage.

Gay marriage is a hot topic right now. Several countries are embroiled in various stages of debating the issue. Many have finally legalized the union, which means that all of the paraphernalia of weddings has a new market. This means that Wizzley actually has two sub-categories for articles about it. The first is under Culture and Society, then Social Issues. I've interpreted this to be the place for all of those Wizzles discussing why gay marriage is even controversial. (I struggle to see what the opposition is here.)

My Archie article is an ideal candidate for this sub-category. Indeed, it's where I originally placed it. It's where it's one day destined to return.

The reason this was great is because it was the only one there. People clicking into that area only had my article to read. It also placed highly in the parent category, as the only representative of its section. But without other articles supporting it, it was more difficult to publicize on tools like Twitterfeed.

I turned to the second option, which is under

Relationships & Family, then Marriage. Gay Marriage here has four more articles around it. I can throw the RSS into Twitterfeed and have them scroll through for nearly a week. Once I moved Archie there, my hits on the article made a sudden upturn. One day, I will write more on the political and cultural side, then Archie can return to where he should be.

Optimizing Wizzley for Twitterfeed

Twitter isn't the only platform for promoting your articles, but it's the one that I've been concentrating upon recently.

When Humagaia wrote about the benefits of Twitterfeed, I paid attention. Those who read the Tips and Tricks for 100 Pages will know that I also fell foul of the rules almost immediately, but it's all sorted out now. Writing the last 50 pages has been the period when I really had the chance to play with this program. I'm impressed. Bursts of internet traffic followed its use. I'm a fan and I'm going to continue to utilize it. But along the way, I've had to tinker with what I write about and where I position articles. Archie was moved for Twitterfeed convenience. But the rest has been in focus.

Twitterfeed will only fetch ten articles at a time. This is great if you have ten articles there, but when you only have one or two, then it's hardly worth the time to upload the feed. My response then was to look at the sub-categories with only a couple of Wizzles in them, then write more. The number of articles in Computer and Electronics suddenly doubled in a short space of time. In History, I homed in on the Edwardian period, disdaining all others, to amass a decent number of Wizzles in there. It's the same story over in Travel & Places, where my solitary article on Cardiff was very quickly joined by another six articles.

The aim is to have at least ten articles in a number of sub-categories. It has already paid off, especially as they are supporting each other. I've seen a jump in readership, which appears to be holding.

Tips and Tricks After 200 Pages on Wizzley

- Published on August 16th 2012

Eight months in and my Wizzley portfolio feels heavily pregnant with potential. But I've not yet given birth to a livelihood. It's coming. So many people tell me that it's coming. Just one final push, and the trickling pennies will start turning into pounds. I can see the interest there. The tiny kicks of more traffic, more clicks. The occasional random buy. But in the meantime, my articles consume the front page; and my tenth Editor's Choice is in the bag.

Reading My Tips & Tricks

Everything that I share with you is true, but they should be placed in context. I am new to on-line writing. Veteran authors may pour the sum of their experience and knowledge into our grateful minds. I can take you on a journey.

As I learn my craft, I stop every fifty pages to record what I have found. It's as much a diary, or a way of remembering myself, than it is a tutorial for those who follow. These are my class notes and my revision. They are the things that I found do work.

If isolation and frustration are the hallmarks of starting out in this writing game; then you don't have to do it alone. Come walk with me.

Fans as a Way of Promoting Your Wizzles

It was the first time that I'd really paid attention to the fan button. It proved to be very illuminating! I noticed a very curious thing. Over the course of two or three weeks, I kept having people become my fans on Wizzley.

I'd dutifully return the favor. They would then 'un-fan' me. Until this moment, I became someone's fan primarily if I liked their work and wanted to keep reading it. Secondly, I'd befriend strangers out of politeness, if they had done the same to me.

The first few times that this fan/unfan thing happened, I dismissed it as my articles not being what they expected. But when it kept on happening, my instinct rang.

I approached the font of all knowledge and wisdom, also known as Sam. She informed me that there was a bizarre (and utterly false) belief amongst some writers, that such practice is good for Google SEO. The idea is that you have more fans than you personally are following. The signal is supposed to be sent that you must therefore be a great writer. However, she did underscore the fact that this is not only bad practice, but it doesn't work. I should imagine that it also ends up ostracizing you from your writing community.

This whole episode did result in me paying more attention to the followers section of Wizzley. I discovered that there are some friendly (or wise) souls, who become fans of newcomers as a matter of course.

It doesn't take a genius to work out why. Become someone's fan and they are very likely to click onto your profile, at least once. They might follow back and then they will receive alerts to your articles. The more fans you have, the more inboxes your Wizzle links are flooding into every day. Each fan is a potential reader. Each fan is someone who might forward links to your article to all of their friends and social networking sites. It's a great and subtle way to get noticed.

Personally though, I haven't changed a thing. I follow those who sound interesting, or whom I befriend; or I return a follow out of politeness.

Promote Everyone's Wizzles in your Social Networking!

Not only is this good for the community and Wizzley, but it might have an unexpected bonus for yourself. Anyone who has been following these tips and tricks will know that I'm using Twitterfeed. This was advice given by Humagaia, which has worked out well for me. I collect my articles together into categories, then use the RSS feeds to post them onto Twitter. But some categories only have two or three Wizzles penned by me in them. At first, I was running them, then just letting the feed drop. That was an error.

Humagaia's second major advice was for us all to raise Wizzley where we can. If people are coming to our website, regardless of which article brought them here, then we all benefit. They might find our writing next. It occurred to me that I could help my fellow authors by running the feed to the category, not just my contribution to it. Ten links are lifted before Twitterfeed stops. Three might be mine, but the other seven are highlighting the work of others on the same site.

That was my altruistic gift to Wizzley as a whole. But then I noticed something which made it beneficial to me too. Wizzley includes 'you might also like' links to other articles in that category. If my own Wizzles are on that list, then that's indirectly promoting them too. It turned into a win-win situation.

Optimal Number of Articles for Wizzley and Twitterfeed

Six for Wizzley; ten for Twitterfeed. That's the minimum number of Wizzles for each sub-category.

Six Wizzles for Wizzley If you have six then every one of the 'you might also like' links will be your own articles. This is only true if each article is at 100% page rank.

Ten Wizzles for Twitterfeed The RSS will only gather the ten latest articles in the feed. It will then produce any new ones, but won't go further back.

Write Often, Write Well

When I was first starting out, a veteran writer told me that the number one tip is 'write often, write well'. If you did nothing else, then that would ensure your eventual success.

What that actually translates to is a lot of hard work. On-line writing is not the easy route to making a living. Apparently it can be, much further down the line, when this all turns into passive income. But that is not handed to you on a silver platter.

First comes the endless hours of writing with no obvious reward. You may take pride in your traffic, and in the readers liking and commenting upon your work, but the main objective can only be taken on faith. As the months have passed at Wizzley, I'm now seeing the benefit in that adage. Write often, write well, has now resulted in some of my very early articles taking off. The same story is being repeated throughout my portfolio. It proves the truth of the earlier conviction of veteran writers that we just have to be patient. It will come.

In the meantime, the hard work has to go on; and with it a further underlining of that precious tip: write often, write well.

Check Older Articles to Keep Them Current

It takes time for these things to mature. You need to make sure that your Wizzles look pristine at the moment that they're found!

I was at a friend's house and wished to check in on Wizzley. Not going through my usual bookmark, I merely typed the name of the site into a search engine. Naturally this gave me a list of links where our site is mentioned, hence I got side-tracked into some reviews. One boldly claimed that Wizzley is like a hybrid of the best parts of Hubpages and Squidoo. I knew nothing of either site, but I did know that some of the owners originated in the latter. I went digging.

Apparently, in Squidoo, if you don't maintain your pages with constant up-dates, you lose your page rank. I wondered if a similar ethos had transferred to Wizzley. I revisited some of my lower ranked and/or older articles; and I'm very glad that I did! But they were merely corrections and keeping things up to date. What about the initial investigation to see if up-dating meant higher page ranks?

Yes, that's as true for Wizzley, as it is Squidoo. Whether that is best practice or a transferred mechanism, I don't know. I chose two Wizzles which were completely under-performing. They both had low page ranks and not a lot of love. I went in and added new content. I messed with the formatting and, in the case of one, I changed the sub-category where it could be found. Then I watched and waited. Both began to climb up the ranks within a day. One has carried on doing so, until it rose from 52% to 84% at the time of writing.

There was nothing wrong with either. No broken links nor out-dated information. They just benefited from a recent edit.

Frequently Asked Questions

Right now, I'm in the happy position of being at the top of the 'Excellent Authors' page; and my articles, without exception, visit the 'Popular' pages at least once. This naturally elicits a lot of the same two questions, asked by various Wizzley authors, turning up in my private message inbox.

Why are you always number one or two on the Excellent Authors page?

I have the most Editor's Choice Awards on Wizzley. That page is solely based on that. You will receive a rosette after you have achieved three Editor's Choices. That will place you in the top tier. Those at the very top have more than three awards. By my observation, it appears that they change position based on a) number of awards and b) most recently given awards.

Until last Tuesday, I was number two on that list, because Sam had more recently received an award. I was given one that night, which moved me to number one. This same organization takes place at each level. Those without rosettes are ordered from those with two Editor's Choice Awards, then one, then 100% author rank and so on.

How can I get on the front page of the Excellent Authors page?

Write often, write well. The Wizzley team are everywhere. If you write something which they consider to be outstanding, then you will receive an Editor's Choice Award. You're aiming for three of them. Don't get despondent if it takes a while though. I've received ten such awards from 200 articles. They are elusive things!

Which is why getting one is such a cause for celebration.

How are your articles consistently taking over the Popular page?

They all hit 100% page rank. The Popular page only deals in the latest pages to do that. This is nothing to do with my Author rank, Editor's Choice nor anything else. Each and every article stands or falls on its own merit. Mine get there because I work hard to ensure my articles hit 100%.

As for how to raise your page rank, I already wrote about that in my first Tips and Tricks. The only thing that I'd add is that 'information' articles tend to get more hits, likes, social network shares and comments than 'sales' articles.

Tips and Tricks After 250 Pages on Wizzley
- Published on September 29th 2012

Every fifty pages, I pause and share all I've learned. This time there's been an emphasis on money-making; and an article that went viral.

Nine months of writing for Wizzley, and this labor of love is beginning to pay off. As my earliest articles have gained some maturity, I've seen rows of pennies turn into double figures. The only trends are upwards - for myself and for the website at large. Behind the scenes, veteran online writers are congratulating themselves. They're in at the ground floor and telling me that we're going to be big.

And this is the month when over 70,000 people read one of my Wizzles in a single day. That was exciting, I can tell you!

Basic Tips and Tricks for Wizzley: Menu Pictures

Add attractive pictures to your article! The most important of all is right at the top, but there are writers who miss this fact.

Over the past few weeks, Wizzley has metamorphosed into a very visual website. Instead of text-based lists of articles, we now have images lining the galleries. The picture that is shown is the one beneath the 'basic data' tag, in the top left-hand corner of our writing templates. It sits on the page alongside the title, tiny and barely seen. But out on the menu pages, it takes on a life of its own.

It is our shop window. It entices readers in to discover our written wares. (And hopefully our displayed monetized products too.) It looks good on sites like

Pinterest, when our articles are circulated by readers. It provides a focal point in an increasingly picture oriented cyberworld. I've seen articles by a handful of Wizzley writers who do not seem to recognize the importance of this. They may add an apparently unrelated or poor quality image, and at times, no image at all. Others may apply the same picture repeatedly, in a way that seems to imply lack of attention, or misunderstanding of the impact this image can have on the success of their articles.

But I'm not an artist, I could be wrong. That is one of the endemic problems with writers. Unless you are extremely talented, most people are one or the other - wordsmiths or artists. The direction of Wizzley asks us to be both, or, at least, slightly competent in the latter.

It's not rocket science though. Websites like Pixabay are full of fantastic pictures, taken by people who know their way around a camera. All we have to do is choose one and add it. Voila! Job done! And it will pay dividends when your Wizzle comes to be displayed. Your work will nestle professionally amongst all of the other shop windows, and may well attract a reader or two.

Basic Tips and Tricks for Wizzley: Profile and Wizzography

On a related point, I was flicking through the authors' pages and also my referral page. I noted that there are some writers who haven't yet completed their profile, nor done a Wizzography.

When it comes to adding an avatar (profile picture), then all of the points above stand here too. An image not only adds color to your page, but indicates to the reader that you have some level of commitment. It just looks more professional. I'm also assured, by those with experience in these things, that it conveys warmth. Readers look into your portrait's eyes, or recognize a familiar avatar, and you feel more real to them. It humanizes you. It makes you close to being a friend. It invites people to read your articles and be more kindly disposed towards you.

Naturally a single picture can't do all of that alone. It's akin to leaving the door ajar, with a big welcome sign attached to it. What they find once they venture inside is up to you.

If an avatar is a subtle 'look at me, I'm lovely, come and read my stuff', then a Wizzography is like taking out a billboard advertizement. I always recommend, to those whom I've referred to Wizzley, beginning with a Wizzography. It tells us who you are. I've read articles and followed people based on what I've read in their Wizzley biography. That has led to friendships too. This is a no-follow area, where you can add as many back-links to your own blogs and websites as you wish. Moreover you are setting out your credentials for all to see.

I've come from an academic background, so I want to see where people are coming from. Why should I trust what this person is writing? What do they bring to the party? The Wizzography is where I find out. If you haven't got one, then you're just a random person on the internet. Why should I care what you have to say, or what you have to sell?

Basic Tips and Tricks for Wizzley: Answer Your Comments!

Have your readers taken the time to write a comment at the foot of your article? Have you taken the time to reply? I'm frequently surprised when I find that comments to articles remain unacknowledged. Possibly the author is a newbie and has not yet mastered the skills of interpersonal online engagement with one's readers.

Perhaps they have not had the chance to check to see what kind of response their articles have been getting.

In order to encourage continued activity on your article, you should make sure to reply to those who took the trouble to add a comment to your work. It is good manners and it makes good sense. Remember, articles on which readers participate actively get recognized by Google. You can write all you like, but it means nothing unless people are reading. That's always been true, but even more so in modern internet etiquette.

This is why authors like Cory Doctorow allow every one of their novels to be downloaded as free eBooks. (If there's no download link, wait on, or scroll down to earlier books. He relies upon fans to convert them, so there's a bit of a time delay.) If you like what he's written, then you'll go back and buy a copy. He's not alone here. Musicians like Grace Petrie do exactly the same. You can listen to every one of her albums and EPs on her website. Fans then click on the purchase button.

This is the future of the internet! This is what our business models now look like. In times of recession, there's less money around, so consumerism is more focused. The age of the customer is back. Your customers are your readers. Ignore them at your peril. Treat them with disdain and they will repay in kind.

On Wizzley, this shouldn't even be an issue. The infrastructure encourages us to respond to each and every comment. Under the 'comments' tab, on your dashboard, you don't even have to visit the page to answer them. The SERPs love articles which have created a buzz. Their algorithms take such things into account, when they are deciding where to rank you. Conversations in the comments indicate a buzz. Again this is reflected by the Wizzley team. What do we call Wizzley articles with lots of comments? Buzzing!

It should also be noted that more comments equate

a higher article rank. If you want to retain any hope of being on the front page, then you have to answer them. In terms of pure volume, your response doubles the number of comments.

Wizzley Algorithm: 100% Means 100%

The site is over a year old now, that's time enough for writers to uncover some helpful tips in the coding. Just a quick note here to emphasize the importance of quality articles on your personal publicity. Every article that I write appears on the front page within seconds. This isn't because I've slipped a back-hander to the Wizzley team, nor that I've done any special favors for anyone. It's because I've worked hard and tried to maintain a high standard on all that I write. There really is no substitute for that.

Write often, write well bears the repeating in every one of these Wizzley tips and tricks that I create. If you do nothing else, do that.

Let me spell out what the Wizzley algorithm does (disclaimer: on observation only). If the majority of your articles are ranked 100%, then your author rank will also be 100%. This is true in a sliding scale down. If the majority of your articles are 1%, then your author rank will be 1% too. Without even checking you out, a casual reader will assume that you're crap. Simple as that.

If you are ranked 90% or over, then your articles appear in the latest Wizzles feed on the front page. There's only three of them at any one time, so it's an ever updating list of the bright and the best on the site at this moment in time. That's a tremendous publicity boost right at the launch of each new addition to your gallery. I've come to expect between 20-50 hits within the first half an hour of one of my articles going live.

Wizzley Battleships! Want to Play Too?

Of course, write often, write well is time consuming. It's another way of saying that you're going to spend half of your life sitting in front of a computer writing articles. Wizzley authors do talk to one another on the forum and, slightly less formally, in private messages. We do break up that hard work with a large dollop of fun!

I can't take any credit for the latest hidden game doing the rounds. That belongs with the irrepressible and cheerfully inventive Jerrico Usher. But I was there at its inception. I 'sank his battleship' and a whole new diversion was born.

As previously mentioned, high-ranking Wizzley authors see their newly written articles appear in the topmost front page feed. As soon as another author posts their Wizzle, yours moves down the list. Three articles later and yours disappears, until it's gained a large enough article rank to appear in the main section. This is our game-play board. It's time to play Wizzley Battleships! Each newly listed Wizzle is your battleship being placed on the 'board'.

The object of the game is to fill all three slots, however temporarily, without another Wizzley author posting an article. If they do then they have sunk your battleships. It's a game which takes strategy and timing. The temptation is to write any old rubbish, so you can get your articles out more quickly. That tactic ultimately leads to failure, as you lose your author rank and you're out of the running entirely.

You know that Jerrico and I are playing. You may join us if you like! Good luck!

Maiden, Mother and Crone - A Private Wizzley Game

I'm probably the only person who knows that I'm doing this, unless some very observant Pagan noticed. That is, until now. The first time it happened, I was quietly amused and quite pleased. The second time, my jaw dropped; then I ran with it.

I'm a Wiccan. I'm responsible for the majority of Wiccan articles on Wizzley (at least at the time of writing). Therefore I'm practically programmed to spot patterns along the lines of the Triple Goddess. The Maiden, Mother and Crone comprise the Three-in-One, one of the most important deities in our pantheon. So what has this got to do with the price of cheese?

In our personal Wizzley galleries, the articles are arranged in a very specific fashion, but it can look quite random. Each new Wizzle pushes the previous one down one place and so forth. After a while, that article will rise again to the head of the middle column; before descending again until its moment to rise to the top of the third. Then one day, I glanced at my profile after posting an article, just to check that all was well. My Pagan sensibilities were pleasantly startled. Right at the top of the page, if you looked with the right sort of eyes, were articles about a crone, a maiden and a mother. The Three-in-One accidentally depicted!

I smirked, told my Pagan friends on Facebook, then promptly forgot all about it. That was until it happened again. Once more, I had not predicted nor caused this to happen. But there it was again. Unless the Lady Herself had a hand in it, then it was purely coincidental. Of course, once I'd noticed it, I couldn't forget it again. Part of me wanted to put it to the back of my mind to see if the Fates would complete the cycle naturally. Would I have written an article about a Maiden at precisely the right time? We'll never know. I couldn't ignore it long enough to find out. I kept checking so, of course, I knew when the requisite slot would be taken.

What I can say is that I was overdue writing a review of *Year of Wonders*, and the protagonist struck me as being the first in the Trinity, despite elements of the rest. However, at the time, I chose to write it then, in full knowledge that it would cause a third Three-in-One configuration.

I'm still doing it. Look closely at my profile gallery and you'll watch that configuration come around time and time again. In fact, my penultimate article, before this one, was a 'Mother' one in order to fulfill that Trinity. I plan to continue doing it until a) I mess up or b) the Wizzley format changes to stop me. It will be interesting to see if I can keep coming up with the articles for it! If you keep watching carefully, you will spot me at it.

The amusing thing is that my Triple Goddess articles appear to have been rather well-received. I was honored with an Editor's Choice Award for that one about Granny Weatherwax; and another 'crone' one elicited rather a lot of comments (the aforementioned buzz!). I have wonderfully kind veteran writers encouraging me behind the scenes. More than one of them highlighted one of my 'mother' Wizzles as evidence that I'm finally getting how to do sales articles. While the original 'maiden' one has already led to commission from Amazon. It's like the Three-in-One really are smiling on my hard work here!

But mostly I'm doing it for two reasons. The first and most important is that it amuses me, while harming none; and an amused Jo is an enthusiastic one, able to write all of these Wizzles for you. The second is accidentally strategic. It is so accidental, in fact, that it didn't even occur to me until KatieM2 posted something to the forum and my eyebrows nearly disappeared into my hairline.

Who Are We Writing For?

Before we rush willy-nilly into producing content for our galleries, it's worth pausing to consider our target audience(s). These are almost the fabled Grail Questions: What is the Wizzle? Whom does it serve? Or why are we writing Wizzley articles and for whom?

Katie's forum post was entitled Demographics. It asked if we should be taking into account all that we know about our readership base. Then should we cater solely for them; or seek to expand interest into other demographic groups? According to Alexa's statistics, the majority of our readers are female with children. They are college educated and aged 25-44 years old. They are reading from their homes.

From my point of view, this was perfect. My cycling through the Triple Goddess was producing a lot of female-centric articles. I was ahead of the game! My refusal to treat my readers like idiots was paying off too. These are college educated. They're intelligent. This would explain why I had so many hits (and sales) on articles which, by all the laws of marketing and SEO, shouldn't even be getting traffic.

However, the statistics are problematic too. They rely upon the readers having an Alexa toolbar installed. Have you got one of them? If not, then you haven't been counted and you don't figure in the demographics. Common sense tells me that there are many male readers here on Wizzley. I am responding to their comments! They're here. Also I've just had the biggest boost in traffic ever and it came from one of the most male-populated sites on the internet today - Reddit*. Where are their numbers in these statistics?

My thoughts here are that, while we take on board these demographics (and ensure that there are plenty of articles in our gallery to welcome those who fit them), we shouldn't ignore everyone else. They're around too and deserve just as much content.

* Information from Alexa again, which states that males are over-represented there.

The Day my Wizzley Article Went Viral

To say that it took me by surprise is an understatement. I think I went into shock! I wasn't even at home. I knew nothing about it until the 'phone call. It was September 16th 2012. The Welsh amongst you will know immediately why I was out and about. This is Dydd Owain Glyndŵr. I'd been exploring Sycharth and joining in Corwen's celebrations. But now I was slaughtering my friend in a game of Risk. (It serves him right for playing me on the anniversary of the day that Glyndŵr declared Welsh independence.) As I took him down, I was called by fellow Wizzley author Paul, a man who is a keen Redditor too. Did I know that one of my articles was on the main page of the Front Page of the Internet? No. But I knew that I was taking Asia and Australasia was in deep peril.

In truth, I didn't grasp the full enormity of this. I thanked Paul for the heads up and told him I'd check it in a bit. I won that round of Risk, then began another. I was soundly thrashed, being over-confident and making noob opening moves. Then I made a cup of tea. Finally I meandered around to logging onto Wizzley and checking my stats. That moment will be indelibly seared into my memory for life. Each time I refreshed the page another 10,000 people had had a look.

I couldn't comprehend it. My mind couldn't grasp those kind of figures. I stared, refreshed and stared. My friend, better known for his wise-cracks and giving no quarter to anyone, quietly commented, "Well done." Then tried to fix these people into my mind by pointing out that

I'd have filled Liverpool FC's Anfield Stadium into over-capacity. And it was still rising. Nearly 80,000 people read my article within a single day.

What was the Result of the Reddit Surge on my Wizzley Traffic and Sales?

At best it's negligible. I may have acquired a few more readers. By a week later, it was like nothing had occurred. The day that it happened passed in surreal accomplishment. Who couldn't be stunned knowing that tens of thousands of people were reading their words? But even then, the more experienced writers here were warning me that there was unlikely to be any monetary benefit in this. Reddit readers are extremely internet savvy and blind to commercialization.

Nevertheless, I did get about twenty-eight Amazon clicks and I made 38c on Chitika! So yeah, I have no plans to retire on the back of it. It's all good, I didn't expect to.

The most visible effect is that I'll be unable to really use my Wizzley or Google Analytics statistics easily for a while. That spike will disappear around March 2013 by my estimation. It's simultaneously highly amusing and a blow to morale. I habitually used those stats to monitor how I'm doing; and to use as evidence in my pep talks to myself. That shouldn't be interpreted as saying that the whole experience was harmful. In fact, it's been very useful. It took me by surprise, caught me on the hop and taught me some very valuable lessons.

Is YOUR Article Ready to go Viral?

Don't ask me which one. I'm referring to all of them. If any one of your Wizzles took off tomorrow, would it be the right one to have done so? Mine wasn't. It had been written very early on, during a Wizzley push for Valentine related stories. It had attracted some attention, but its readers numbered in single digits each week. I'd frankly ignored it, letting it grow a little authority, though I had plans to revisit it before next Valentine's Day.

I'm sure that you can see my error right there. When this article took me by surprise with such a surge in traffic, I wasn't even at home and in a position to spruce it up! None of the little pointers in presenting products were in place. Nor any of the things that I've learned in formatting. The top section looked messy. The articles that it linked to were similarly out-dated and amateur. The main sidebar link was an unrelated one of Katie's!

In short, it was a little like special visitors turning up, when you haven't done the housework for a week and the washing up is piled into the sink. I was ashamed; but determined that it would never happen again. Since that date, I've been on a regime of tidying up my Wizzles category by category. I've been applying all that I've been taught and rendering them safe to go viral. This is naturally a very 'just in case' kind of thing, but also necessary for more run-of-the-mill, passing footfall kind of visitors. Any updating automatically gives a boost to your article's ranking too.

So are ALL of your Wizzley articles in a position to go viral right now? If not, you really should do something about them, or end up knocked as off balance as I was.

Sales Articles Tips for Wizzley and Elsewhere

I can't claim any credit for most of these tips. Some are observation, but the majority are kind veteran writers helping me out. If you're anything like me, then you have a passion for writing. You're here because you love crafting words into meaningful articles. But that isn't putting the bread on the table.

I'm British. I find this whole consumerism thing a little distasteful, but it has to be done. At least it does if I'm ever going to make a living out of this. What I can say is that September has been a bit of a turning point for me.

I've always had a lot of interest, especially with Amazon and Zazzle affiliate products, but not a lot of bites. I'm suddenly getting them now, still only a trickle, but more frequently than before.

Moreover, it's not the 'sales' articles, that I've been experimenting with recently, but the 'information' articles that have been around for months that are providing the purchases. Time really is a major factor here, as people have been telling me from the start.

Here's a list of what I'm keeping in mind, as I present items for potential revenue:

Is the product relevant to the article? Shoving in any old crap just to monetize your writing won't do anything.

Are you actually selling anything? This one came from Katie, who pointed out that I'm very good at setting up sales for everyone else. But then not writing sales oriented articles to capitalize on it. Her example was my Bigfoot obsession, which tells you all about Sasquatch, but then leaves it open to sales vultures to plonk a perfectly monetized article in the middle and 'steal' all of my potential revenue. My response was to quickly write some 'sales' type articles about Bigfoot. I do listen!

Are you focusing on the product too much? If you're keyword stuffing fluff around the edges, your readers will know. They are intelligent people (see demographics above).

Can people find it? Sam has led the gang of people extolling the virtues of Market Samurai. It's one of the best (possibly actually number one) programs out there for finding keywords and key phrases. These are the things that people actually search in order to find articles like yours, and the products linked from them.

Are you publicizing it? Humagaia is the greatest advocate of more traffic equates more potential customers. It sounds like pure common sense doesn't it? Yet you'd be amazed how few people promote their articles in social networking and other areas. Get the word out there, so that you can attract readers.

Humagaia was also the first person to tell me about a product presentation formula, which has since been repeated by others: Say what it is; tell people to buy it; tell people why they should buy it. Others have called this 'presenting, then solving a problem'.

Free Software to Help with Wizzley Sales

Would I be a geek worth my salt, if I didn't share this with you? The first is useful to all, and the second for those outside the USA.

Wizzley monetizes using four main affiliate links. They are Amazon, Zazzle and AllPosters. Then we can throw into the mix the trillions of sites on the VigLink database. So you've written a glorious article and now you're looking for relevant products. How do you find them? I have no idea, but I know how I find them. I use Firefox as my browser. Amongst the Add Ons for that is a free program called 'Add to Search Bar 2.0'. Mine is optimized for Wizzley.

You can find it by following these steps (if you're on Firefox; if not, awww.)

* Click on Firefox, in the top left-hand corner of your toolbar.
* Click on 'Add Ons'.
* Select 'Get Add Ons'.
* Search 'Add to Search Bar 2.0 by Dr Evil' in the search bar located in the top right hand corner.

* Install it.

Alternatively, go to his open source page and download it from here. Then any site with a search area can be added. Just click in the place where you'd search, right-click and select 'add to search bar'.

I started with the default searches that come with a Firefox installation anyway. Then I added YouTube and Pixabay. The one that says 'Amnesty - Google Search' is actually Google images, but with advanced settings showing only public domain/free for commercial use images. That's my video and picture content for my articles sorted. Below come the big affiliate sites on Wizzley, followed by the VigLink merchant search. The stores after that are all ones which I know are affiliated by them. I merely type my product search in once, then click down the list to see what everyone has got on offer to match it.

The second freebie solves a problem for Google users outside the USA. We want to check its shopping pages, so we can locate stores which stock the items that we wish to display. But Google refuses point blank to let us search outside our own countries. For example, my Traditional Welsh Dress article was starting to lack viable places in the USA to buy the costumes. Unusually, I had no joy hunting through the stores that we generally use, so I wanted to look further afield. I clicked on Google's shopping search and typed in 'Traditional Welsh Dress'. I got loads! Well, I would. I'm in Britain, which is where this outfit comes from! But could I find it in America?

I had no idea. I could type in Google.com, but the coding would throw me back into Britain. I would try searching 'Welsh dress in America' and it would only show me British stores which shipped to the USA. There was only one thing for it. I had to stop Google knowing where I was located, so that I could actually get search results meaningful to me. I used Proxify to conceal my IP address from Google's cookies, forcing its search engine to look at

my query instead of myself. It worked.
    Incidentally, that will work on any site. Not just the big one.

Tips and Tricks After 300 Pages on Wizzley

- Published on November 8th 2012

Making a living by writing online isn't all about typing words in blank boxes. That's just the substance of it. There are all of those little things that you can do in the background to increase the likelihood of your articles being read. SEO and positioning, formatting and picking topics that are bound to do well. If you're just a beginner, then the bombardment of advice can feel overwhelming. This series is me pausing every fifty pages to journal what I'm doing and what I learned. May it help you as much as it's helped me.

You Are Writing For This Time Next Year

Since I first began writing online, veterans further down the road have been unanimous in saying the same thing - it takes time before you see a return on your hard work. Some of those projections make depressing reading. No-one makes anything in their first year. It can take two years for cents to turn into dollars. It can take four or five years before you're making anything like a living wage.

Of course, there will always be the lucky ones, who fall upon the right topics at the right time, or who bang out the 'sales' articles for a quicker return. Yet the latter risk losing the long term rewards, as items fall out of fashion before maturity is reached. From this melee of dire warnings and advice, it was Jerrico Usher's voice which rang most clearly for me. "You're not writing for today," he told me. "You're writing for this time next year, or the year after."

You couldn't get much clearer than that! By keeping his words in mind, you are looking forward to a time when your work will have settled into the search engines, and gained enough readers to have sprouted organic back links. Moreover, it's a great check to ensure that your article is evergreen. There's many years' earning potential in those.

On a psychological level, not expecting any return for a year or two will also stop you feeling despondent, when the riches haven't rolled in immediately. If they do, then that's a bonus worth cheering. Incidentally, this whole thing about having patience is true. I've been amazed just recently how many of my articles have suddenly come to life - in terms of readership and traffic - after months of sitting there doing nothing much. It's like the internet only just found out about them.

I'm in the Money Tra-la-laaa I'm in the Money

Yes! You can make money on Wizzley, as long as you put in the effort and wait for a bit. It's been the million dollar question since I first arrived. Forget about stats and party games, are you making any money? The bottom line has to be the concern of even the most passionate writer. We might love to get our words out to a waiting cyber-crowd, but we also need to put bread on our tables.

For those just starting out, it looks like easy money, right up until the moment when it patently isn't.

A single article, or a handful of articles, thrown out to the masses has as much chance of funding your retirement, as your teenage kids have of recording the world's best selling record. It could happen. Elvis Presley, The Beatles and Justin Bieber seem to do alright. But the reality is that it takes time to see some return on your online writing. It can take months. It's the hugest test of faith ever to keep on churning out the articles, and hoping that it'll all be worth it; and one day earn hard cash.

Moreover, this is fertile ground for paranoia. What

if it's only the site's owners and a few favorite writers who make the money? What if you're simply the industry's equivalent to cannon fodder or slave labor? Doing the work and then being thrown on the scrap heap, before gaining your reward. I had the faith and I lived through the paranoia. The money is now trickling in. Note the trickle. It's gone from months of zeros, through to cents. Then the single digit dollars began to appear. A couple of months later - BAM!

Seemingly overnight, old articles suddenly started making money. It's not mega amounts, but it's in the low double figures and it's steady. I won't be buying a tropical island any time soon, but it's all enough to prove to me that the old wisdom was correct. Write often, write well, don't give up and it will come. Just like everyone said all along.

'Seeding' Articles Between Wizzley Categories

One of the wonderful things about Wizzley is the massive choice of sub-categories in which to write. As the website is barely over a year old, there is the opportunity to be here at ground level. Today's Wizzley's authors are the ones with free rein in filling them all. Imagine how that will look, once the rush begins in earnest (as it already has).

However, lonely Wizzles in a category aren't going to do much for your bounce rate. I've already advocated writing at least two, but now I've worked out how to do even better.

All articles posted here retain their same URL wherever they are located. You can constantly move them from category to category, until you find the perfect fit. Plus that huge choice of categories means that you have plenty of places to park them.

My tip is to find yourself a center of operations, then blossom out from it. It's like letting a mighty tree cast out a seed for a sapling.

There will be a general, catch all category, which allows you to corral appropriate Wizzles until you have a fair number. Ten is good for Twitterfeed. But amongst their number, you could add two or three which narrow down the field. They will mature nicely amongst those generally related articles. But they will also form the basis of the colonization of another sub-category later. Once moved, they will take with them all of the readers attracted by the article's maturity in search engines. That's a much better foundation than a lone, newly written Wizzle in a pioneer's category. This can be done the sensible way, or in reverse, where you send out 'pioneer' articles into other categories, then bring them home.

There may have been some puzzled faces when I placed a Wizzle about women in the American Civil War into the Victorian Era category. It's not that it doesn't fit, but US History may be a much better fit for the topic. I agree, and one day The Women Who Fought in the American Civil War will indeed be moved over there. But today is not that day.

The reason is that I already have plenty of established articles in the Victorian Era category. They are gaining maturity and helping me develop my authority as a history writer. By being grouped together, readers attracted by one article may easily find the others too.

Meanwhile, I have nothing else in US History. My lone article about it is more likely to be read in the lesser category, than in the perfect fit. Over the weeks, I'll gradually add to them, until such time as I can move them over en masse. By then, they'll have achieved their own maturity and will transfer that into their new and better location. This can also work in reverse, as I recently discovered.

This Halloween, I wrote many, many articles about the different costumes available for your spooky events. At the same time, I was so interested in Bigfoot, that I'd filled that category here on Wizzley almost single-handedly. The two naturally merged into Halloween costumes for both Yeti and Sasquatch. They were placed into the Halloween costumes for adults section. Still there was some crossover. In writing the Yeti outfit article, I realized that the Bigfoot category did not include one about this legendary creature. So I wrote it. Linked up with the Yeti costume article, in the high visibility sub-category of Halloween in October, it did very well.

But then the holiday was over and hits began to fall off. I judged it time to take 'Halloween' out of the title, and move both the Yeti and Sasquatch costume Wizzles over into the Bigfoot area. The result astounded me. Alone of all my Halloween costume Wizzles, these two not only didn't lose internet traffic after the big day, but gained more readers! Moreover, every one of my Bigfoot and Sasquatch articles registered the same boost.

That's what I call a successful reverse seeding!

Don't Put Too Much Pressure on Yourself

There is already enough of all that by sheer dint of the fact that you're trying to make your way as an online writer!

Every guide you will ever read about making your living by writing online will state the same thing. It's not easy money. You will have to work hard to carve your niche in the market. I've done this myself. How often have I written, in these tips and tricks, that you should write often and write well? It's still great advice, but it can go too far. There is a thin line between pushing yourself with motivational techniques, and setting yourself up for failure.

People are always telling me that they admire my stamina on Wizzley. They wonder how I can create so many freshly written articles, so consistently and in so short a time. The answer is that I'm approaching it as a gamer. I level up with these articles. I hit my targets and run to the next. But first I have to create the levels to achieve. Nintendo never did pair up with Wizzley to do it for me.

So here are the motivational targets, which just stacked up and up:

a. Every fifty articles, I stop and take stock. You are reading the results of that one right now.

b. Every sixth article conforms to the relevant aspect of the Triple Goddess.

c. I've set myself a challenge of having written 366 articles on Wizzley by December 16th 2012, exactly a year after I arrived here.

d. In order to maximize 'sales' articles, I'm following the advice of most of Wizzley, when they point out that holidays and festivals are huge selling times. Hence the dozens of Wizzles for Halloween and Christmas, and yet another for Bonfire Night. Such things have deadlines, and I'm horribly aware that those are months in advance.

e. I've joined a Pinterest paranormal group, which has created a huge amount of exposure for my ghost stories. So much pressure there to keep on producing them.

f. On the subject of promotions, there is the Twitterfeed technique, which does fulfill its promise of increased internet traffic. But optimization involves at least ten articles in each sub-category.

g. The massive milestone of 300 articles required something special, so I planned it in advance. A lot of research and work went into my gift to myself and Wizzley. As a historian, I really wish that it had existed from the moment I walked into this community. Writing About History on Wizzley exists now.

h. Also as a historian, I have the entire of time and space to plunder for articles, at least where the human story is concerned. Which means that I'm constantly looking ahead for major historical anniversaries, then writing about them in advance of the commemorations.

i. Posting two articles in a row triggers the competitive spirit that has me wanting to beat Jerrico Usher at Wizzley battleships.

j. The look of my profile is a concern. I try not to have too many 'sales' or 'information' articles in the same rows. Mix and matching for the win!

k. And I'm also keenly aware that Wizzley has a competition running right now, which I haven't contributed even one article towards.

Add all of these things together and the questions need to be asked - What ails thee? Whom does it serve? Because way beyond targets now, it's a big ball of pressure, which needs to be pricked. I've got to the point of writing what I 'should' instead of what I want to. Such an approach is fatal, when you're already under stress. Plus a little silly too. I had an article planned in my head, which would have gone out a week ago, had I not been sticking so strictly to my schedule. Another Wizzley author wrote about it yesterday, gazumping me to the post.

When motivational techniques and a gamer's approach become a heavy weight of 'must' and 'duty', then they are no longer doing their jobs. The trick is to strike a balance. Write often, write well indeed, but not to the point of burn out and tears. It's a trick that I'm still in the process of learning.

One More Motivational 'Game' at Wizzley

At least with this one, I don't have to actually do any work! Perhaps this is the way forward for my gaming instinct. Every Wizzley author checks their statistics. Even if we weren't after the confidence boost of knowing that there are actually readers, we'd be looking for clues as to what we should be writing about. I've kept the stamina levels going, on a daily basis, by checking out those ordered by seven days; and picking a number.

Originally it was ten, then fifty. Now it's 100. I count the number of articles that have attracted over 100 readers in one week. Then I rejoice and pat myself on the back, if they amount to more than ever before. Currently my record is twenty articles with over 100 readers in a week. I don't beat myself up if that falls below, but I congratulate myself heartily if it goes above. A new entry for the Wizzley hiscores.

Tips and Tricks After 350 Pages on Wizzley
- Published on December 4th 2012

It's possible to write nearly sixty Wizzley articles in a month. I know because I just did it. Don't expect too much from this latest Tips and Tricks. It came around so quickly!

As a reasonably new online writer, I've been on a steep learning curve. You are seeing it in action. Advice comes from all angles, from kindly professionals and websites, through feedback from friends, and from readers. It's hard to know which of it is right, which of it is wrong, and what depends upon the writer. Every fifty Wizzley articles, I pause to take stock. It's part journal, part sharing all I know. Welcome to the 350 page edition!

Writing a Book? Put your Research on Wizzley!

The eBook market is huge and many writers are transferring their time to producing them. This doesn't mean that you can't also contribute here.

Since the beginning of time (well, last January, but it does feel like a long time ago), fellow Wizzley author Sam has been telling me to write a book. She's not alone. There's a bit of a queue for that, but all of the others are pointing at fan fiction. I kept telling her that I'd think about it. I did think about it, but not with any actual ideas behind it. Then I finally had one.

Has no-one thought it suspicious that I suddenly appeared fixated on a very narrow moment in Jacobean history? There are those who would consider it a general interest in history; and they'd be right. There are others who might note that it all started around Bonfire Night, so was quite topical. They'd be right, as would the people observing that between Anonymous and the popularity of *V for Vendetta*, that particular history is always topical. But there's another word for a close examination of everything to do with a specific thing. It's called research.

I've had my idea for my eBook. Sam can stop nagging me. I've even asked around those looking for less formal fan fiction. The feedback went along the lines of, 'I would read the &%$& out of that!!' So yes, I'm writing it. In the meantime, my research notes are all articles on Wizzley. I hope that you're enjoying them!

I'm in the Money! I'm in the Money!

In November 2012, eleven months after joining Wizzley, I made over $100 for the first time. This is the bit which everyone (new and prospective writers especially) is really interested in. It's not my 1337 gaming tips. It's taken me eleven months to get into triple figures in a month here. The veterans did it much sooner. Bear in mind that I'm new to writing online overall; and I'm doing it without Google Adsense, which is apparently the internet's cash cow.

Anyone who's read all of the previous Tips and Tricks will have followed my progress with money-making. From the earliest days of rebellion against 'sales' articles, to learning how to love them, it's been an exercise in working it all out.

The buzz has always been that 'sales' articles do better financially than 'information' articles. I didn't want to! Back in the Tips and Tricks for 100 pages, I even resorted to singing *West Side Story* songs in protest. The experienced writers maintained that it was the way forward. Well, I've been there now. I have data. I know much better what is going to work for me. ('It isn't true, not for me! It's true for you, not for me!' Sorry, *West Side Story* attacked again...)

As you can probably tell by all of the Halloween and Christmas Wizzles, I've discovered that 'sales' articles can be quite lucrative. They were all right. Every single person who kindly repeated the mantra to me when I was young and foolish.

Up to a point.

Did I sell a lot of Halloween costumes? Yes, I did. Not enough to buy a tropical island to retire upon, but there was a smile on my face as I checked Amazon. But they are not where the bulk of my earnings have come from. The top two articles in my 'module clicks' tabs are both 'information' ones. The most consistently lucrative Wizzle, in actual sales, is most definitely an 'information' one. (I really didn't expect to sell a thing off it! And it's been steady for three months now.) The biggest single sale that I had from any article at all was an 'information' one.

Maybe I'm an anomaly, I don't know. My experiences have definitely been swimming against the tide of the perceived wisdom passed down by our wise, tribal elders. Please note that I'm not saying that my 'sales' articles have yielded nothing, they have; but my 'information' articles have monetized much better so far. Obviously this is an unfolding story, so watch this space.

Wizzley Sales Article Tips

I'm still learning here. It's all very new to me. But I have picked up a few this month.

Wizzley doesn't add the price by default. I'm experimenting with removing the title too. You can have that in your module title, which looks much neater. But by removing all information from the module, you're also encouraging people to click on Amazon, Zazzle or wherever. Otherwise they only have a picture and your waffle to go on. Surely that's the name of the game here?

Don't just repeat everything that you've read on Amazon, Zazzle etc, then rehash it into an article. It's boring and you're contributing nothing new to the wealth of knowledge. Why should a reader come to you for recommendations? They could just cut out the middle person and search those sites for themselves. Be original, so that you earn your commission.

The bigger the picture, the more enticing it looks. If the British government think that they can stop cigarette sales by hiding them behind counter shutters, then there's obviously something in seeing = buying. Extrapolate the marketing information and think big on your product images. On the other hand, we're all still buying cigarettes...

Watch your keywords and phrases, as gathered in the stats page for each article. They will tell you what people are actually searching to find your Wizzle. This is good for both 'sales' and 'information' articles, because each keyword or term is a potential title for another Wizzle.

Fifty-Six Wizzley Articles in Less Than One Month

It's all part of my gamer's mindset; and the challenge that I set myself to write the equivalent of an article a day on Wizzley. Trust me to choose a leap year.

Back in the summer, I needed motivation. The prevailing wisdom was that the more you write, the better your chances of making it as an online writer. Part of that is simply common sense. Getting your name out there means that more people recognize it. That's one way to attract readers to keep returning. The regularity of articles may mean that you become a fixture in someone's daily routine.

One of my proudest moments was when a work colleague admitted that she's bookmarked Wizzley. On her commute each morning, she checks the news, then pops here to see what I and the others have come to tell her about today. It passes the time until she reaches her bus-stop.

I also recall reading Problogger Darren Rowse's views on keeping on writing. He said that each article is a chance to find a reader. Each sales module is one more opportunity for that reader to buy a product. To my mind, it's like ensuring that you win the lottery by buying as many lottery tickets as you can afford. Only here, you pay in time and determination; and it's a little more guaranteed than the luck of the draw.

None of which helps, when you're back in front of a computer in the middle of summer, taking great leaps of faith that one more article is worth it.

I'm a gamer. What can I say? I need levels to attain and boss monsters to pwn. Veteran writers might waffle on about buying opportunities, quality, quantity and SEO, but when I think gold coins, I usually have to be pressing 'B' and knocking a wall down to ping them. I set myself the challenge of writing 366 articles in one year. It probably owed more to Mario than Darren Rowse, but I'll deny that if you meet me in a professional capacity.

Two friends did the mathematics. They told me straight what this would entail. It was impossible, because I'd already messed it up by only writing 20, 19 and 18 articles in April, May and June respectively. Ok, so not impossible, but it would involve having no life and screeching head first into burn out; plus risking learning how to hate writing. I took it all on board. Well, I didn't take any of it on board at all. Except the word 'impossible', which a wise woman once told me should be believed in multiple figures before breakfast each day.

Always better at taking advice from Alice than mathematicians, I began writing, and writing, and writing. You can see the results on the screenshot from my Excel spreadsheet there. Only sixteen left until 366! (And twelve days to go.)

So why am I telling you all of this? Partially because these Tips and Tricks have always been a journal too; plus the bragging rights. But mostly because I've just written fifty-six Wizzley articles in a single month. I've demonstrated that it can be done. Judging by the likes, comments and other indicators, they weren't shabby either. I tried hard to maintain the quality all along.

Those beginning their journey on Wizzley often quail under how long it takes to write an article here. There's making it look pretty, placing modules, conjuring headers and finding images, above and beyond the actual writing.

Fifty is the magic number. After fifty articles, your percentage cut of the profits goes up. In short, I'm mentioning it as it sends out a signal that you potentially could hit that major milestone in less than a month of registering at Wizzley.

Good luck!

Wizzley Gamer Levels

Do you have a gamers' mindset too? Let me help you out with some skill levels to attain! People think that us gaming types don't pick up any transferable skills from all of those hours spent pwning pixels. They're wrong.

In a MMORPG that I've devoted many hours to, there's a distraction and diversion called Achievement Diaries. Each area has an attendant list of tasks or accomplishments. Complete them all and you get bonuses, plus an item to wear. There will be some reward in donning it.

Here on Wizzley, we can have Achievement Diaries too. The bonuses are implicit. Unfortunately, we don't get the special item of clothing, unless we can persuade

Ragtimelil to work out how to create one. It's not beyond the realms of possibility. We talked her into felting a Runescape Canifis hat!

Noob Tasks

Write five Wizzley articles. Your reward is that your Wizzles will hereon be automatically set to 'follow'. No moderator will look at it before Google, Bing and all of the rest do. You're certifiably a professional Wizzley author!

Get an Editor's Choice Award. Your reward is zOMG! You have an Editor's Choice Award! That article has the 'wow' factor, as determined by a member of the Wizzley team. It will gain much more publicity, as it will spend a long time on the front page of the whole site.

Attract over 50 readers every day for a week. This is all of your articles combined. Your reward is that people are reading your articles.

Make a sale on Amazon. It can take anything from days to months for this to happen. It's cheating if you get your Mum to buy something. Your reward is the commission.

Make a sale on Zazzle. See above.

Make a sale on VigLink. See above, this includes anything sold in an eBay module, as that's monetized through VigLink.

Make a sale on AllPosters. See above. And if you're anything like me, this is the one that you're going to really struggle to cross off your Noob Tasklist!

Intermediate Tasks

Write fifty Wizzley articles. Your reward is that your monetization percentage will go from 50/50 to 55/45 in your favor! The team behind Wizzley will cry, but you'll be quids in. Bread on the table, that's what we're aiming for here.

Get a second Editor's Choice Award. Your reward is zOMG! You have TWO Editor's Choice Awards! This has all of the bonuses of the first one, but in addition, it's moved you one step closer to the elite three ECAs. That's just boosted your position in the Wizzley author boards.

Attract over 100 readers every day for a week. This is all of your articles combined. Your reward is that more people are reading your articles. It's all building from here!

Make regular sales on Amazon. It can take anything from months (maybe years) for this to happen. But it's the biggest indicator yet that everything is working as it should. Plus it's a much shorter leap from here to making a proper livelihood, than it was from one or two sales to this point.

Make regular sales on Zazzle. See above.

Make regular sales on VigLink. See above, this includes anything sold in an eBay module, as that's monetized through VigLink.

Make regular sales on AllPosters. See the note on the Noob Tasks, then sob.

Advanced Tasks

Write one hundred Wizzley articles. Your reward is that your Wizzles will firstly and rightly be the bragging rights. This is huge! Well done! Then it'll be that your monetization percentage just leapt to 60/40 in your favor. ChefKeem will need a stiff drink, but it's happy days for you.

Get a third Editor's Choice Award. You now have a rosette next to your name on your profile. Every fellow author and reader will know that you're a quality writer and that your work is worth reading. You'll be on the first or second page of the Wizzley authors, and you have the potential to be at the very top of the list! Very well done!

Attract over 500 readers every day for a week. This is all of your articles combined. Your reward is that your articles are patently maturing very nicely. They are being read long after you've written them (unless you've got one going viral!). This is precisely what this game is all about. You're doing brilliantly.

Make a livelihood on Amazon. It will take years for this to happen. Your reward is that technically you can retire now.

Make a livelihood on Zazzle. See above.

Make a livelihood on VigLink. See above, this includes anything sold in an eBay module, as that's monetized through VigLink.

Make a livelihood on AllPosters. See above. See the previous notes. Remember that it's better to laugh than cry. Good luck!

Elite Tasks

Write one thousand Wizzley articles. Your reward is that no-one has ever done it before. Currently the most prolific Wizzley author is Ryank. You would own the hiscores, if Wizzley had any. Plus all of those articles would be bringing in readers and potential shoppers too.

Get ten Editor's Choice Awards. No-one will ever be able to knock you off the front page of the Wizzley authors. Plus it's only ever been done once before. *takes a bow*

Attract over 1000 readers every day for a week. This is all of your articles combined. Your reward is that your articles are seriously doing their job. You have the authority to attract readers; you have made your name. Now you just need to be patient and keep going. Very well done!

Get stinking rich through Amazon. This might never happen. If it does, then you don't need me to tell you what your reward is here!

Get stinking rich through Zazzle. See above.

Get stinking rich through VigLink. See above, this includes anything sold in an eBay module, as that's monetized through VigLink.

Get stinking rich through AllPosters. See above. See all of the previous notes. Enjoy a wry smile.

Tips and Tricks After 400 Pages on Wizzley

- Published on February 28th 2013

After a year on Wizzley, I've amassed a lot of articles which are starting to mature. It's fun watching to see which ones will suddenly wake up!

My Wizzley Tips and Tricks is as much a journal, as it is passing on information. I'm learning my on-line writing craft, so pausing every fifty pages to record what I know seems sensible. It doubles as a way of reminding myself of the things I've known, and letting those following me see real data, alongside the tips. It's something that I wish I had had, when I began this journey. I've been here a year now. It's been (and remains) fun.

The Long Grey Days of January

After the soaring Christmas rush, everything came back down to Earth with a bump. What goes up must come down. That's how the old saying goes, doesn't it?

Back in early autumn, I recall Jerrico Usher gushing on the Wizzley forum about how the approaching festive season has boosted internet traffic. Everyone was coming to buy presents for the holidays; and those who weren't had been chased indoors by bad weather. They were all surfing the 'net and finding us. It was truly marvelous! Every time I checked, someone had bought something else on Amazon, eBay or Zazzle. VigLink was booming. I was making more in one month than I had in six previously. I'd finally arrived.

Then Christmas passed and January was upon us. Grey days drizzling outside my window. Too cold to venture far, too poor to pay for the petrol to travel any great distance. No-one was buying much on-line. The gift giving season was over and we were all skint. Suddenly that profit from Wizzley took a nose-dive and left us all feeling depressed. The bills weren't going away either.

It's my first real January as an on-line writer. I felt myself soul-searching to see if this was really the path for me. I loved the writing, but if it wasn't paying its way, then I had to find a job which did. I know I wasn't alone there. Wizzley authors were taking it in turns to raise each other's spirits.

It was HollieT who provided the golden insight for me. She told me to forget comparing January's stats with December, but to look back to last January. Now how did it look? Tremendous actually. I'd more than doubled my income! As for unique readers, there was an increase of 3,366% between last January and this. Back then I was averaging 30 readers a day, this year I'm averaging over a thousand. Success on anyone's terms!

January and February dips for us all. It's how we view it which keeps us going. On the plus side, traffic and sales were great from September to December! And they're hardly shabby right now.

Splitting Up Wizzles for Bounce Rate Happiness

Do you say twenty words when you could say one? Do you waffle on forever? No? Well I do! I've got monstrously long articles accordingly.

There are pros and cons involved in writing long articles. A big plus is that you get a lot of keywords in there for potential readers to search and find. A major downside is that those long walls of text seem intimidating. Wizzley has a rule that you can't publish less than 400 words per Wizzle. There is no upper limit that I've found (and I've surely reached high enough by now!). But long articles for the sake of long articles may be doing you a disservice. If your reader has plowed through 5000 words, which don't really say anything, then they are unlikely to make that mistake again. Keep it short, unless there is still a story left to tell.

There is another alternative too. Splitting your articles up into a series will help reduce your bounce rate. This is something which I did to great effect (according to Google Analytics) when I told the story of St Patrick recently. They were all long articles and they could have been a single one. But dividing them into four, published over four days, turned it into a serial. People came back to learn what happened next. People read to the end of one and clicked to read the next. My bounce rate was low on all!

Pretty as a Picture on Wizzley

How much thought have you given to your Wizzle's thumbnail? This is the image representing your article all over the internet! They say a picture tells a thousand words. That's true on Wizzley too, but mostly it just looks good. Pictures break up huge walls of text, which can make a page look attractive enough to read. A surprising number of readers do skim-read, before deciding whether to commit the time for a proper perusal. Plenty of images help with those snap decisions.

But what picture should you choose? For text modules, it doesn't matter too much. As long as it's relevant and a nice image, then it's not worth worrying too long over your choices. It's the main thumbnail which requires a little more discernment. Your Wizzley article has to stand out amongst an array of others. A good title will do that, but the real eye-catcher is the image.

Until you delve a little more deeply, Wizzley categories are basically a load of pictures. They are your 'hooks' to grab readers. They'll see the image, read the title, if they're still interested, they'll read the blurb underneath. Then they're in. I spent some time just looking over the front page of Wizzley. I took notice of which images caught my eye and why my gaze drifted over others. I realized how important color was in this situation. So many authors opt for tons of white - usually an Amazon product against a white background - I was filtering those out.

Since then, I've taken care to add a splash of color. Even if I'm writing a 'sales' article, I'll go for the most colorful option in the images available. If there's no option but to use one full of white, I'll nip into GIMP or Paint and add a border. I'm not the most artistic person in the world, but it makes my articles stand out. You can write the most wonderful article in the world, but if it hasn't been read, who will know? The thumbnail picture is like the bait on the end of your hook. Make it a good one!

Examples of how I've chosen thumbnail images:

- The cake is a lie article was headed by a screenshot. It filled more space and looked more colorful than the products on their own.

- The *Someone Comes to Town, Someone Leaves Town* book review had the front cover pasted on top of an orange background. It covered all of the white, which was originally there.

- The majority of portraits of Hannah Snell are in black and white. Perhaps the worst of the bunch was the only one in color. But I selected it, because the bright red stood out and, well, it was in color.

Should You Make Your Own Thumbnail Images?

This is one way to get noticed! There will be nothing else like it on the internet. But have you got the talent? I'm not very artistic. Sometimes I can take a decent photograph (and they end up on Zazzle), but mostly I'm more wordsmith than graphic designer. For this reason, I might add a border or copy and paste to produce a picture, but you won't find me creating my own from scratch. I just haven't got the talent.

If you have, then by all means go for it! But if, like me, your limits look like something a three year old could best in Microsoft Paint, then you need to think about it a little more. Getting it wrong might cause potential readers to overlook your article, but worse still, they might prejudge it badly. A bad image might equate, however unfairly, a badly written article.

By the same token, Wizzley is designed to look good. There are professionals within the Wizzley team tinkering to see what works. (Check out Nightowl's biography for a start!) For those of us with no artistic vision at all, then this is a great benefit. It stops us cluttering our Wizzles until they look like a bad Geocities or MySpace come-back. Unless you know what you're doing, then it's probably best to back out of trying to pimp up your pages too much!

Things to consider when choosing an image:

a. Is it relevant to the article?

b. Does it represent my article, as an ambassador for the words inside?

c. Does it stand out when surrounded by other thumbnails?

If you have a winner, then attach it to your work. Every little bit helps!

The Wizzley Community is Wonderful

Working together, we make the whole of Wizzley great. Readers arrive and that's of benefit to us all. Back when I was a new writer on Wizzley, there was a big push for creating a community. It came from the people themselves. Naturally ChefKeem, NightOwl and the rest of the Wizzley team were thoroughly in support.

Veteran writers like Humagaia led the call. He pointed out the importance of us all making friends, leaving comments on each other's work, extending a welcome to newcomers. He also noted that Wizzley is a very young website. The rest of the internet needs to know about it perhaps more than each individual author. The rationale was sound. The greater the site's reputation, the more readers will venture here. Our own work will receive a boost accordingly. Plus it just makes Wizzley a nice place to be.

I've always been a team player better than a lone wolf. I run with the pack and look for the well-being of all. I know I'm not alone in that! Suddenly we were all chatting on the forum, linking each other's articles from our own, putting both Wizzley and the reader first. The latter should be our priority anyway. It all led to a wonderfully supportive community, which didn't seem to suffer the same bad feeling as in other forums.

Fast forward a year and tight friendships have been made. There's nothing clique-y about it. It's mutual and it's a lovely place to be. Wizzley itself is stronger for it. It's created a great environment in which to write, and to which to invite our writing friends.

I saw that in action this month! And how I

applauded.

A Mass Exodus from Suite101

This is where I began, but February 2013 brought some unprecedented and rather surprising news. Since August 2011, I have been on Suite101. I worked my way up to Feature Writer, before such titles were scrapped. It was the first freelance writing platform that I worked on. For that reason, it will always hold a fond place in my heart. I received a lot of early help from its community; and it was on Suite101 where I first heard about Wizzley.

Unfortunately, the site has struggled post-Panda. That affected my traffic and income too. After getting off to a flying start, writing one of the earliest reports on Occupy Wall Street, it all seemed to wither. I was writing a lot of news articles, but Suite101 gave up its Google news accreditation. Good friends immediately jumped ship. I dithered and dallied, until a fellow writer gave me some good advice. She told me that she understood my loyalty, but in this game we can only have loyalty to ourselves. Nothing else puts bread on the table and pays the bills. I followed Christian Dörr into Wizzley.

Nevertheless, I've still kept a kind of presence over on Suite101. It may have been an occasional article, or an e-mail with friends, but I was still there. Then, in February 2013, came the announcement that Suite101 was changing again. The new model didn't include paying writers for their future articles. Suddenly a whole community of people were looking for a new home. I had just the place! I spent a whole week over on Suite101, answering questions about Wizzley, as people evaluated their options. Then, to my utter glee, I watched many of them choose to come here.

It was a strange moment. It was like two friends from different parts of your life meeting up; or a couple of extended families gathering at a wedding. I found myself getting anxious - what if this group of friends didn't like that group? Of course, I needn't have worried. As soon as the influx was obvious, Paul (a Wizzley author) created a forum thread welcoming in the newcomers from Suite101. The Wizzley community flocked to say hello. It was beautiful. I was so glad I was here to witness it.

As for those coming in, my Wizzley inbox was buzzing for days. One by one, the ex-Suite101 writers thanked me for bringing them here. It was better than I'd even made it sound, which is a rare thing indeed in this game!

Community Feeling at Wizzley

Unsure how to leap right in and become part of the gang here? It's ridiculously easy. Everyone will welcome you.

Here are a few tips to get you started:

Involve yourself in the Wizzley forum. A good starting place is the 'Newbies Say 'Hi" area, which is precisely what it says on the packet. Another great, and highly informal, place to chat is right there at the bottom: 'Chatter Away, Friends!' It's where all kinds of silliness ensues, as well as deeper discussions and more profound personal news.

Follow other authors and comment on their work. They'll soon reply and a new friendship is born!

Privately message someone. I've lost count of the number of friendships that I've made here, because a kind reader (and fellow author) PMed me to tell me about a typo. Random acts of kindness rule the day. Or if you stumble upon a bit of information, which plays right into another author's field of expertise, then give them a heads up. Even if they already knew, then it's nice to have the contact.

Suggest a collaboration. If you're writing about something, which would benefit from a sister article written by somebody else, then ask them about it.

Highlight another author's work in your sidebar or within your Wizzle itself. This helps the readers, if the article is relevant, and boosts the reputation of Wizzley accordingly.

Thank You!

This guide could not have been possible without the army of friends and family, who have kept me sane throughout its conception and writing. Special thanks therefore go to the following:

To Freya for the cover art; Sareyva for beta reading this book, all my Wizzley articles and everything else that else I care to write; Paul, Ember and Lisa for keeping the stamina levels up and dealing with all my moments of doubt and fear; Kate, Liam and all else who take the time to comment upon my articles. You and I all know the debt to which I owe you.

To the wonderful Wizzley community, who have always been so generous with their time, encouragement and advice. Particularly to Achim and Sam, who urged me to finish this guide.

Thank you all.

www.ingramcontent.com/pod-product-compliance
Lightning Source LLC
Chambersburg PA
CBHW051215170526
45166CB00005B/1916